Trash Cash, Fizzbos, and Flatliners

A DICTIONARY OF TODAY'S WORDS

Trash Cash, Fizzbos, and Flatliners

A DICTIONARY OF TODAY'S WORDS

by Sid Lerner, Gary S. Belkin,
and The Editors of the
American Heritage Dictionaries

HOUGHTON MIFFLIN COMPANY
Boston · New York

Library of Congress Cataloging-in-Publication Data

Lerner, Sid.
　　Trash cash, fizzbos, and flatliners: a dictionary of today's words / by Sid Lerner, Gary S. Belkin, and the editors of the American Heritage dictionaries.
　　　　p. cm.
　　Includes indexes.
　　ISBN 0-395-64021-0. — ISBN 0-395-64020-2 (pbk.)
　　　　1. English language — New words — Dictionaries.　2. English language — Slang — Dictionaries.　3. Americanisms — Dictionaries.
I. Belkin, Gary S.　II. American Heritage Publishing Company.
III. Title.
PE1630.L44　1993　　　　　　　　　　　　　　　92-33849
423'.1—dc20　　　　　　　　　　　　　　　　　　CIP

Printed in the United States of America

Book design by Robert Overholtzer

AGM　10 9 8 7 6 5 4 3 2 1

Contents

Acknowledgments

The authors are grateful for the new words, kind words, and guidance from Robert Gordon, Robert C. Fischer, F. Peter Model, Morton Stark, Bonny Hart, Samuel Newborn, Robert Sternau, Robert B. Costello, Barbara Cooper, Greg Peterson, Allan Lang, Helaine Lerner, Joan Rechnitz, J. Bud Feuchtwanger, Harold I. Drucker, Daniel Gardner, Les Werkstell, James A. Longo, Richard B. Stephens, and Lisa Horan.

Introduction

Keeping up to date with the English language is a task that never ends, as anyone who compiles and edits dictionaries can confirm. Life keeps changing, and English hustles to keep up with new coinages, reinventions, and reshaping of the language. Science, technology, politics, communications, computers — all keep developing and requiring fresh vocabulary to fit the new developments. Slang and street language are in a perpetual state of unpredictable novelty and recycling that manages to keep insiders in the know and outsiders mystified. *Trash Cash, Fizzbos, and Flatliners: A Dictionary of Today's Words* captures this language on the wing, before it can vanish or before it has become established and recorded in standard lexicons. It is a dictionary of the moment, intended as a useful and entertaining supplement to the familiar dictionary kept in the home, office, or school.

Every new edition of a standard dictionary contains its share of new vocabulary that has withstood the test of time. For example, the *American Heritage Dictionary of the English Language, Third Edition*, published in 1992, has 16,000 entries or meanings added since its previous edition. Since a standard dictionary is published in a new edition only at intervals of some years, and since space within the dictionary is limited, there is for the most part no room left over for the ephemeral. A bright new coinage will have to stay around for a while to justify its inclusion. Short-lived slogans, slang, and catch phrases may perish unrecorded.

This is where *Trash Cash, Fizzbos, and Flatliners: A Dictionary of Today's Words* makes its special contribution: it takes a snapshot of newly minted language, analyzing and defining it while it is still fresh. The authors, Sid Lerner and Gary S. Belkin, along with their corps of citation-gatherers, have explored books, magazines, newspapers, pamphlets, advertisements, catalogs, product labels, and any other reading matter that came to hand in their search for new vocabulary. They have listened to radio and television and to conversations on buses, subways, trains, and planes. They have picked it up in sports arenas and at rock concerts and computer conventions. They have accessed information-retrieval databases.

The hardest job has been exclusion, rather than inclusion. Sometimes a term seemed too made-up for a specific occasion or circumstance to warrant its inclusion (for example, **hairshift**: a shift in discussion of a political candidate from the candidate's political views to the candidate's hair style, or **flag bait**: patriotic imagery, as of the stars and stripes, used to attract votes). Other terminology generally omitted is in the specialized vocabulary of obscure or highly technical fields. In a book like *Trash Cash, Fizzbos, and Flatliners: A Dictionary of Today's Words*, with a limited number of pages, a balance must be struck between the serious and the frivolous.

We have tried to present a cross section that demonstrates the constant vigor and originality of English vocabulary building. There are many quoted examples of usage in this book. Pronunciations, respelled in a simplified and easy-to-understand system, have been provided when it seemed they would be useful. The practices of traditional lexicography have been applied throughout to clarify the definitions. A very valuable feature of the book is its Index, divided into several subsections to give a quick overview of new words covered in particular fields.

The editors will be glad to hear from readers who wish to comment upon an entry in this book. Suggestions for new entries, accompanied whenever possible by printed examples of actual usage, will be most welcome. They can be sent to Sid Lerner, c/o Reference Department, Houghton Mifflin Company, One Beacon Street, Boston, MA 02108. Unfortunately, it is not possible to give either compensation or credit for such contributions.

Trash Cash, Fizzbos, and Flatliners: A Dictionary of Today's Words, is, finally, meant to be fun to read. We hope it will on many occasions provide the meaning for a new word you have just come across. But just as often, we hope you will find it simply a source for happy browsing.

Robert B. Costello, Executive Editor
American Heritage Dictionaries

A Dictionary
of Today's Words

A

abb *noun*
(*Surfer Slang*) An abnormal person; weirdo.

A-Beijing virus *noun*
A virus strain that causes a type of flu (**Beijing flu**) that has a higher than usual death rate and is somewhat more resistant to standard flu shots than other strains.

ableist language *noun*
Language that is presumably insensitive to disabled or handicapped individuals, such as saying to a blind person, "Do you see what I mean?"

abortion pill *noun*
See RU 486.

abortuary *noun*
A clinic where abortions are performed. A term used by opponents of abortion. [From *abor*tion + mortu*ary*]

ABS *noun*
An automobile safety feature that uses a computer to control the wheels during emergency braking to prevent them from locking. [Abbreviation of Antilock Braking System] Also called **anti-locking brakes.**

accelerated death benefits *noun*
See LIVING NEEDS BENEFITS.

acceptional child *noun*
A variant of the phrase "exceptional child," indicating a youngster with special problems that need attention in the school or in clinical settings. This variant spelling is intended to stress the idea of acceptance, as opposed to the presumed exclusionary implications of exceptionality.

ACE inhibitor (ays) *noun*
Any of a class of drugs (technically, angiotensin converting enzymes) that are used in treating high blood pressure and have recently been designated by the FDA as dangerous for pregnant women. [From **A**ngiotensin **C**onverting **E**nzyme]

acoustical oceanography *noun*
A new branch of oceanography that deals with the sources, physics, and distribution of sound waves in ocean waters. The acoustic phenomena under the ocean's surface reveal a wealth of climatological and historical information about the planet earth. See MICROBUBBLES.

active-optics mirror *noun*
A flexible mirror used in ground-based reflecting telescopes. Using an adaptive optic technology, these mirrors respond to information from a light sensor, bulging and dipping to compensate for the natural distortions in the light reaching it from faraway planets and stars.

addiction medicine *noun*
A new branch of psychiatry specializing in the treatment of addictive disorders, such as substance abuse or compulsive gambling. The American Board of Psychiatry and Neu-

rology now offers a certification examination for psychiatrists who wish to be recognized as specialists in this new field.

ADHD *noun*

A syndrome that chiefly affects children and is characterized by short attention span, easy distractibility, and physical restlessness. [Abbreviation of Attention Deficit Hyperactivity Disorder]

adult gamedy (GAY-muh-dee) *noun*

A late-night, sexually charged television program, as "Studs" or "Personals," that is an updated version of the older dating game format.

advance directive *noun*

A written instruction by a medical patient stating in advance what kind of medical treatment he or she wants or does not want in the event the patient becomes incapable of communicating intentions and wishes during the course of treatment.

AFM *noun*

A new instrument that uses an atomic-sized tip that resembles a phonograph needle to read a surface by touching it and then tracing outlines of its atomic structure on a computer screen. [Abbreviation of Atomic Force Microscope] Also called **atomic force microscope**. See OPTICAL MOLASSES; OPTICAL TWEEZERS; STM.

African snail *noun*

See GIANT AFRICAN SNAIL.

Agenda 21 *noun*

A major environmental cleanup plan for the 21st century that has been the subject of new and expert analysis, strong public support and criticism, and political maneuvering over the past ten years. Various efforts by the 12 nations of the European Community, the US, and many of the Latin American and Third World countries have yet to establish a date or method of implementation.

AG*SAT *noun*

An educational satellite-delivery system, named for the Agricultural Satellite Corp. of Lincoln, Nebraska, a consortium that operates the system for 37 of the nation's land-grant universities. According to the *Wall Street Journal*, in 1991 about 70,000 people, using AG*SAT, took courses at home ranging from agricultural marketing to hog-manure management, from schools such as Pennsylvania State and Iowa State. See DISTANCE EDUCATION; LEARNING CIRCLES.

AirLand Battle *noun*

A multi-force military strategy, integrating naval, air, and land forces, deployed successfully for the first time during the Persian Gulf War. Developed as a theoretical model by the Pentagon in the 1970s and 80s but never before tested in combat, the AirLand Battle strategy positions the thrust of an attack against the enemy's rear lines and support reserves, with the goal of making the enemy's front line vulnerable to attack by weakening its underpinnings from the rear.

Alar *noun*

A trademark for a chemical preservative (daminozide) used on fruit. It has recently become the source of controversy after being identified as a potentially carcinogenic agent. Products marketed as "Alar-free" are not supposed to show any traces of this preservative.

alternative dentation *noun*
False teeth. A bias-free term.

alternative rock *noun*
A category of rock music that includes a blend of metal, heavy metal, and mainstream pop and is generally performed by regional bands, such as "Nirvana," that achieve some degree of fame by their signing to large labels or sudden and unexpected success of a regional album.

American Ecowriter *noun*
A new type of pencil, manufactured by Eberhard Faber and marketed as environmentally friendly, in which the barrel is made from recycled newspaper and cardboard instead of wood and the ring around the eraser is recyclable. Also called **Ecowriter.**

AMT *noun*
A minimum tax that certain taxpayers have to pay, based solely on income and earnings and without regard to allowable deductions. [Abbreviation of Alternative Minimum Tax]

amyloid beta protein *noun*
A toxic brain chemical that accumulates in concentrated plaques in the brains of people suffering from Alzheimer's disease.

ANI *noun*
A business telephone service that automatically accesses the appropriate customer record associated with a calling number. For example, if you call your stock broker from your office phone, as soon as the broker answers, your portfolio file, which is keyed in the system to that phone num-

ber, is retrieved from the computer and displayed on the screen. The practical value of the service is in its speed in automatically retrieving the correct account at the instant a call is being answered. [Abbreviation of Automatic Number Identification]

animal companion *noun*
An alternative designation for what is traditionally called a "pet." Also called **companion animal.**

animalist *noun*
An advocate for animal rights.

animal lookism *noun*
A bias toward protecting, pampering, or adopting members of attractive animal species rather than those of less attractive species. See BIOCENTRISM; SPECIESISM.

animatronic toy *noun*
A toy or game featuring CD-I technology for high image and sound quality. Animatronic toys are a growing category of new play products for children that is being "spurred on by the success of Nintendo," according to *Toy and Hobby* magazine. See CD-I.

Anonymous Call Rejection *noun*
A new telephone service that will automatically disconnect callers who try to mask their telephone numbers from receiving systems such as Caller ID or ANI. See ANI; CALLER ID.

antenna shop *noun*
A retail store in Japan that is run by manufacturers for the sole purpose of introducing new product ideas to consumers for their reactions (as reported in *Advertising Age*)

An antenna shop does not have products available for sale, unlike an outlet store, which has manufacturers' merchandise for sale at a discount.

anticipointment *noun*

A term coined by television executive George Schweitzer to describe "what happens when a television network sells expectations to a major level, achieves something less than that, and leaves everyone disappointed."

anti-locking brakes *noun*

See ABS.

anti-slasher law *noun*

A law aimed at controlling the distribution and viewing, especially among minors, of excessively violent videotapes, as *Friday the 13th* and *The Texas Chainsaw Massacre.*

anti-stalking law *noun*

Legislation, already approved in several states and before legislatures of many others, prohibiting the persistent following or harassing of one person by another.

appointment television *noun*

A television programming term descriptive of viewers who plan in advance to watch certain programs, as opposed to those who uncritically watch whatever is on at any time. Appointment television viewers are considered a more sophisticated audience group, one that is highly desirable to marketers.

appropriation art *noun*

Art created by photographing photographs appropriated from magazines, advertisements, and other media sources. See REPHOTOGRAPHY.

arabidopsis *noun*
A small weed of the mustard family that has shown possibilities recently as a foundation for the laboratory production of PHB, a biodegradable plastic. See PHB.

arachibutyrophobia (AR-uh-ki-BYOO-ti-ro-FO-bee-uh) *noun*
The fear of peanut butter sticking to the roof of one's mouth. The word turned up on a class-time news and information program for high school students, on Channel One. It was presumably blended for the occasion from *arachis oil* (peanut oil), *butyrin* (a fatty acid), and *phobia* (fear). See CHANNEL ONE.

archetypicalism (ahr-kuh-TIP-i-kuh-liz-um) *noun*
A design philosophy that transcends any given style and suggests instead that things, such as buildings, furniture, and appliances, should indicate clearly what they are used for: a writing desk, for example, should suggest the image of a person writing at it.

architectural crisis *noun*
The ramifications caused by a hidden flaw in the architectural, or technical, design of a computer hardware component, such as the central processing unit (CPU), that ultimately can lead to major incongruities in performance, especially in the computer's operating system.

arcs *noun*
An extended television story format that enables an actor to develop a character over several hours rather than the usual 60 minutes. The scripts are "written as a string of mini-series, which in the TV script-writing business are called arcs," reported Moira Farrow of the *Vancouver Sun*.

"Hill Street Blues" and "St. Elsewhere" are two early examples of the form.

area denial weapon *noun*
A cluster bomb causing great localized damage.

ARM (ahrm, AY-ahr-EM) *noun*
A mortgage in which the interest rate is tied to a financial indicator, such as the prime rate or treasury bond rate, and thus fluctuates over time as conditions of the economy change. [Abbreviation of Adjustable Rate Mortgage]

Armenia *noun*
A former republic of the Soviet Union that is now an independent republic.

artificial reality *noun*
A computer technology consisting of hardware and software interacting in real time with a user who creates changes in a multimedia-generated environment. An artificial reality system generally consists of hardware, such as stereo headphones and a screen lodged in a face-covering helmet or in goggles, that affects the user's sensory system; input devices, such as special sensory gloves in which movement of the hands controls the environment; and a computer system for overall control. Also called **cyberspace; virtual reality.**

artware *noun*
An artistic medium that is based on advanced computer technology and combines state-of-the-art computer hardware and software, with multimedia extensions, such as TV, audio, and light shows. Film, television, advertising, and the fine arts have all shown the influence of artware.

Asian gypsy moth *noun*

A plant pest that is more destructive than the more familiar European gypsy moth and is destructive to more than 600 varieties of trees, plants, and shrubs. Only recently discovered in the US, Asian gypsy moths are currently the targets of extensive airborne spraying in areas of the American Northwest.

asteroid defense *noun*

An early-warning, $50 million plan proposed by a government-appointed team of scientists to create the first census of asteroids in space that could potentially strike our planet. "Six ground-based telescopes would be built around the globe to scan the heavens and provide warning of impending danger in time enough for work to begin on interceptors to deflect the asteroid," wrote William Broad in the *New York Times* of the asteroid defense. See EARTH-CROSSING ASTEROID; KILLER ASTEROID.

astral projection *noun*

A hypothetical process wherein one's soul is regarded as leaving one's body temporarily and departing into another's body or into an ethereal world.

atomic force microscope *noun*

See AFM.

Auroville *noun*

The first ecological city, located on a rural plateau along the subtropical Coromandel Coast of South India. Founded in 1968 by Mira Alfassa, Auroville has been hailed as the city of the future, combining various alternative urban and social development concepts and space-age technologies that purport to allow people to live harmoniously with their natural resources and with each other.

AutoCut VCR *noun*

An electronic device, available in Japan, that when installed in a VCR can edit out commercials while recording from television. The device, not yet available in the US, works by recognizing the difference between the stereo broadcasting of the commercial and the monaural sound of the television program.

autofacturing *noun*

A word blended from *auto*mation and manu*facturing* to describe the full range of activities of an automated factory, from computerized acquisition of materials to the robotics of loading the finished product on a truck. Autofacturing has become increasingly attractive to makers of products ranging from automobiles to computers.

auto mall *noun*

A retail enterprise that is a cross between a mall and supermarket, with cars, vans, and trucks as the only products. Auto malls are springing up around the country, especially as a sluggish car market makes dealerships eager to explore new selling methods.

automated attendant *noun*

A computerized robot switchboard and directory assistance system used in voice messaging. See VOICE MESSAGING.

available seat mile *noun*

An airline unit of computation for one aircraft seat flown one mile, whether occupied or not.

B

babe lair *noun*

(*Slang*) An apartment used by a man of wealth and power for the purpose of seducing women. [From the use in the film *Wayne's World*]

babelicious (bay-buh-LISH-us) *adjective*

(*Slang*) Beautiful; gorgeous; sexy. [Blend of *babe* + *delicious*, made famous through the film *Wayne's World*]

Baby Bell *noun*

Any of the seven regional telephone services (Nynex, US West, Inc., BellSouth Corp., Ameritech Corp., Bell Atlantic, Southwestern Bell, and Pacific Telesis) created by the antitrust decree of 1982 in which the monolithic AT&T (*Ma Bell*) was divided into the smaller regional companies.

baby buster *noun*

(*Slang*) A person born after the baby boom of the mid 1960s. Also called **buster**.

babycise class *noun*

An exercise class for infants emphasizing swimming and other motor activities.

Baby M laws *noun plural*

A general designation for laws regarding surrogate motherhood (the mechanism by which a woman bears a child for another person or couple, usually as a result of artificial insemination). Baby M was the infant in a precedent-setting New Jersey surrogacy case.

baby wrangler *noun*
In advertising and television, a person who coaches children to perform in commercials.

backmasking *noun*
A technique in audio recording by which information is concealed through normal play, but is audible and intelligible when the program is played backward. Backmasking has become a subject of occasional controversy since a number of rock groups have been accused of using the technique to record "Satanic" messages on some of their tracks.

bad hejab (hee-JAB) *noun*
Inappropriate Islamic dress. See GOOD HEJAB.

bag biter *noun*
(*Slang*) One who causes a problem, as for an organization.

Bagdadi (bahg-DAHD-ee) *noun*
The Georgian city formerly known as Mayakovsky.

baidarka (bye-DARK-uh) *noun*
A fabled kayaklike vessel originally made of animal skins and bone and used by the Aleuts. The vessel was recently rediscovered and reconstructed by George Dyson, son of Princeton physicist Freemon Dyson.

balance billing *noun*
A practice in the health care field of charging a patient more than what Medicare or private insurance will pay for a treatment, visit, or service, the patient being billed for the balance.

balanced account *noun*

A conservative investment strategy involving a portfolio composed of both stocks and bonds that proves less volatile and risky than stock-only accounts. See WRAP ACCOUNT.

BANANA *noun*

Resistance of almost all communities to landfill construction and other undesirable land uses, such as waste disposal or nuclear processing. [Acronym for **B**uild **A**bsolutely **N**othing **A**nywhere **N**ear **A**nything]

Barney *noun*

(*Surfer Slang*) A stupid man. [From the 1960s television cartoon show *The Flintstones*]

base *verb*

A term used in rap music that is roughly equivalent to "argue."

basic brown *noun*

An individual who has minimal interest in environmental issues and would be, on the whole, unwilling to spend more money for products and services simply on the basis of their being environmentally sound. [Derived from a study by the Roper Organization]

basket *noun*

A new trading product that allows investors to buy or sell all the stocks in the Standard & Poor's 500-stock index in one trade. "Baskets have some similarity to futures contracts on the S&P 500, but those contracts do not involve the delivery of shares and expire at a specified date, at which time they are settled in cash, based on the level of the S&P 500 at the time of expiration." (Floyd Norris) Also called **stock basket**.

baubiologie *noun*
(Of a building's environment) Affecting the health of the occupants in a particular way. See SICK-BUILDING SYNDROME.

BaylorFast *noun*
See OPTIFAST.

beam up *verb*
(*Slang*) To experience a crack-induced drug high. An urban street term, especially of the Northeast US.

beat sheet *noun*
A detailed outline for a film or TV show providing a scene-by-scene description.

bedienung (beh-DEEN-ung) *noun*
A German term now used internationally in travel bookings, meaning that the tip is included on the bill.

Bedoon or **Bidoun** (bi-DOON) *noun*
A member of a nomadic population living in the border areas of Iraq and Kuwait. Not to be confused with the more traditional Bedouins, the Bedoons have no national identity or land they call their own, nor any specific cultural, national, or social identification.

Beeb *noun*
A nickname for the BBC, the British Broadcasting Corporation.

Beemer *noun*
(*Slang*) A BMW automobile.

beer goggles *noun*
(*Slang*) Loss of judgment caused by drunkenness. A campus term.

Beijing flu *noun*
See A-BEIJING VIRUS.

Belarus (BELL-ah-roos) *noun*
The former Soviet republic of Belorussia, which is now an independent republic.

Beltway *noun*
The area in and around Washington, DC, with particular regard to the political decision-making powers and influence inherent in its population. ". . . he is derided, by the conventional wisdom that emanates from inside the Beltway, as a fearful ditherer who hasn't even been able to assemble a competent political campaign." (Marjorie Williams, *Washington Post Magazine*)

Beltway bandit *noun*
An opportunistic lobbyist or consultant operating within the Beltway.

bereavement fare *noun*
See COMPASSIONATE FARE.

Bermuda plan *noun*
A travel plan providing hotel accommodations with full American breakfast included in the basic rate.

Bernoulli box (ber-NOO-lee) *noun*
A removable high-density computer disk drive that combines a large storage capacity with plug-in portability. Named after the Swiss physicist Daniel Bernoulli, the drive utilizes principles of aerodynamics and hydraulics to allow the drive's read/write head to float on a cushion of air above the disk, protecting it from sudden mechanical jolts and electrical changes.

be sword *verb*
(*Slang*) To relax. An urban street term.

bias-free *adjective*
Of, relating to, or expressing a neutral, nonjudgmental point of view, as in "bias-free terminology."

bifftad *noun*
(*Teenage Slang*) A rich kid. [From the names *Biff* and *Tad*]

Big Blue *noun*
A nickname for IBM, the International Business Machines Corporation.

big time *adverb*
To an extreme degree; completely, as in the sentence, "The candidate went on to deliver a speech that made clear what we suspected: that he is clueless, big time."

big white phone *noun*
(*Slang*) A toilet bowl used for throwing up during a drinking binge. A term used especially by college students.

Billings mucus method *noun*
A natural birth control method in which a woman measures changes in the cervical mucus to determine periods of ovulation. See NFP.

binge eating disorder *noun*
A psychological condition, related to but symptomatically different from anorexia and bulimia, that constitutes a new category of eating disorder. It is characterized "by frequent, uncontrolled and often hours-long eating episodes during which a person often consumes more than 2,000

calories, the amount a person would need for an entire day,"
according to science writer Jane E. Brody of the *New York
Times*.

bio bundle *noun*
A hybrid security in the biotechnology research and development field that attempts to balance considerable upfront research costs with opportunity for growth. A Wall Street term.

biocentrism *noun*
A doctrine that the earth should be viewed as a resource for all living things and not just human beings. The most doctrinaire holders of this view believe that it is even wrong to kill disease-producing bacteria, since they play a part in the ecological balance of the planet.

biodiversity *noun*
Diversity of plant and animal species in a given region (such as the tropical rain forest), as in, "This practice is causing a decrease in the area's biodiversity."

biofarmer *noun*
A farmer engaged in the cultivation and production of biologically based alternative sources of energy. Current examples would include algae farming and bacteria farming, both of which produce the alternative fuel hydrogen.

bioleaching *noun*
A mining technology that mimics natural oxidation and weathering of minerals through accelerated methods. With bioleaching technology, bacteria digest natural ore deposits, turning the unseparated and useless compounds found in mines into viable oxidases suitable for commercial pro-

cessing. Bioleaching has most recently been used in gold mining.

biomagnetic *adjective*
Of or relating to magnetite (magnetic) crystals found in the cells and tissues of different life forms that, according to Dr. Joseph Kirschvink, might account for the possible influence of strong electromagnetic fields on human health.

biopic *noun*
A movie or television film based on the life of a notable figure. "Columbus is quickly established as a lusty, playful and self-assured man-with-a-vision whose life, in time-honored biopic tradition, is an uninterrupted series of lively events." (Lisa Nesselson, *Variety*)

biorational approach *noun*
An approach to pharmaceutical development and testing that uses advanced biological and crystallographic techniques to advance understanding of the implications of a drug's effects and possible dangers.

bioreserve *noun*
An area that is set outside ranching and farming lands in order to help maintain a viable ecological balance among the human inhabitants, the flora, and the fauna of the area. A part of a movement called **New Conservation,** the bioreserves are seen as natural buffer zones for human residents, tourists, and wildlife.

bioseries *noun*
A television biographical series, usually in consecutive weekly installments, that presents an ongoing story of a famous person, such as ABC-TV's portrait of Elvis Presley as a young man.

Biosphere 2 *noun*

A much-publicized experiment in biosphere living. A biosphere is a human-made sealed structure resembling a greenhouse and designed for the occupants' self-sustaining existence within by simulating the biological processes of the outside world. The Biosphere 2 (our Earth is considered Biosphere 1) comprises a little over three acres, housing 3,800 species of plants and animals, five climate zones, and eight human subjects. It is the first full-scale commercial effort and was built at a cost of over $150 million. It was inaugurated on September 26, 1991, with much fanfare and the expectation that its eight crew members (four men, four women) would remain sealed in for two years.

biphobia (bye-FO-bee-uh) *noun*

An irrational fear of bisexual people.

bird *noun*

A telecommunications satellite.

Bishkek (BISH-kek) *noun*

The capital of Kyrgyzstan, formerly known as Frunze.

bite moose *interjection*

(*Slang*) Used as an equivalent to "get lost."

black box *noun*

A contemporary style of small-theater design featuring movable seats and stage, simplicity of form, straight lines, and characteristic black walls.

blacked out *adjective*

In airline and train travel, of, relating to, or being a time when special lower fares and other prices do not apply.

black hat *noun*

A person involved as a villain in a political scandal. For example, in referring to the Iran-Contra investigations, political columnists Evans and Novak argue, "To put white-hat Weinberger on trial at this late date to face charges based on testimony from black hats who have entered guilty plea bargains would look like a travesty." See WHITE HAT.

black mayonnaise *noun*

(*Slang*) Black sludge found on the bottoms of bays, oceans, harbors, and streams. The sludge is a combination of sewage, pollutants, and natural waste substances.

blading *noun*

The sport of skating with in-line roller skates. See IN-LINE ROLLER SKATE.

bleaching *noun*

See CORAL BLEACHING.

blitz *noun*

See ROADBLOCK.

blocking *noun*

A new telephone service that allows a person placing a call to avoid being identified by a Caller ID system on the recipient's phone. See CALLER ID.

blow up *verb*

(*Slang*) To make a lot of money quickly, usually by selling illegal drugs. An urban street term.

bone *adjective*

(*Slang*) Useless, false, or foolishly wacky: "Don't give me no bone excuses." An urban street term. [Reported by Ilene Rosenzweig in *Street News*]

boogie board *noun*
See HYDROSPEEDING.

bootstrapping *adjective*
Of, relating to, or constituting a new series of analytical statistical techniques designed to reduce error and increase accuracy. Used primarily in large-scale computerized data analysis, bootstrapping methods have become the methods of choice among government agencies and state-of-the-art scientific laboratories.

Borking *noun*
The process of subjecting a Supreme Court nominee to very close scrutiny, especially over past decisions and statements. [Named after Robert Bork, whose Supreme Court nomination was derailed during hotly contested Senate hearings in which his legal philosophy was severely challenged]

Bosnia and Herzegovina (BOZ-nee-uh; hurt-suh-go-VEE-nuh) *noun*
A former republic of Yugoslavia that declared its independence in March 1991. The capital city is Sarajevo.

bottoms-up research *noun*
Fundamental investment research that includes studying annual reports in depth, visiting the competition, talking to customers, and holding intense discussions with management and administrators, all with a view to learning anything that will add to or detract from the accepted market value estimate.

box tonsils *verb*
(*Slang*) To kiss passionately; play tonsil hockey.

BP
Abbreviation of Bermuda plan.

brain birth *noun*
The biological stage at which integral brain functioning begins; for humans, about 70 days after conception.

break-out *noun*
The period at a business meeting or seminar when the group disperses into smaller workshops, discussion groups, or brainstorming sessions.

brew pub *noun*
See MICROBREWERY.

BRI *noun*
A health problem associated with specific buildings and their indoor environments. [Abbreviation of Building-Related Illness] Also called **building-related illness**. See SICK-BUILDING SYNDROME.

bridge line *noun*
A line of designer-collection clothing that costs about half the price of top-of-the-line collections and is intended for the bridge market. See BRIDGE MARKET.

bridge market *noun*
Clothing customers who want quality-name clothes that are reasonably priced.

broadcast fax *noun*
A facsimile machine technology that allows a user to send a fax message simultaneously to multiple recipients.

Bubba *adjective*
(*Slang, often considered disparaging especially by Southerners*) Of or relating to Southern white males and the constituency they are alleged to make up. It has been used

frequently in expressions such as "Bubba county," the "Bubba vote," or the "Bubba factor in politics," all referring to the Southern white vote. Recent objections to its usage have been noted by journalists such as Roy Blount, Jr., a Southerner himself: "New York columnists," he wrote, "toss around the term 'cracker' awfully loosely, and now Bubba is taking over as an ethnic term. There's no other ethnic group that you could use such a slur about so lightly."

bubble *noun*
A quirk in the 1986 revised tax code that has become the source of much controversy. To discourage married couples from filing separately, the combined tax rate rises from 15% to 28% at $32,450, to 33% on taxable income between $78,400 and $162,770, and then drops down to 28% on income above that level.

bubble team *noun*
A college basketball team that has a marginal win-loss record and is trying to play its way into the NCAA tournament.

buck *verb*
(*Slang*) To fire a gun at someone, as in, "We bucked that S.O.B. last night." An urban street term.

buckyball *noun*
A spherical molecule of carbon containing interlocking structures of hexagons and pentagons, named after R. Buckminster Fuller, the originator of the geodesic dome. These carbon molecules are believed to hold great potential for superconductivity, among other new technological uses. Also called **bucky; buckminster-fullerine; fullerine.**

buff *adjective*
(*Adolescent Slang*) Cool; terrific.

building-related illness *noun*
See BRI.

bulk up *verb*
To undergo rapid growth, as in, "Since the government approved the drug, shares of XYZ Company have indeed been bulking up."

bullcrit *noun*
Discussion or criticism of a book, play, film, or other artistic undertaking without the experience of having read or seen it. People who bullcrit rely on the media coverage, critical reviews, word-of-mouth views, and news commentaries, from which they form their opinions and judgments about the work.

bummed-out *adjective*
(*Slang*) Being lackluster or half-hearted, as an athletic performance or event.

bump CD *noun*
A new type of certificate of deposit that allows the depositor to change to a higher rate once during the life of the CD. Also called **bump up.** See RISING-RATE CD.

bump racing *noun*
See MOGULS RACING.

bump up *noun*
See BUMP CD.

bundling *noun*
A disreputable campaign contribution practice in which corporate officials coerce their employees to make individ-

ual contributions, which are bundled together as one large corporate gift, presumably to buy influence with Washington decision-makers.

bungee jump (BUN-jee) *verb*
To engage in bungee jumping.

bungee jumping *noun*
A sport in which a person leaps from a high platform, such as a bridge, hot air balloon, or crane, using an ankle harness tied to a thick rubberized, elasticized set of cords (**bungee cords**), which are in turn attached to the jumping platform. Free-falling to a predetermined descent point, the elastic-action bungee cords cause the jumper to bounce up and down like a yo-yo. When the bouncing stops, the jumper is hauled back up to the platform.

burner *noun*
(*Slang*) A gun; firearm. A street term.

burn-out *noun*
(*Slang*) An unmotivated child who spends more time hanging out than being in school, according to a 1991 survey of New Jersey high school students by *Asbury Park Press* writer Jeanne Jackson.

bush master *noun*
A native, as of a tropical or extremely remote region, who is a trained professional in the recognition and collection of the plants, seeds, and shrubs used by local shamans (medicine men) in their healing rites. Bush masters have become a focus of Western medical research in recent years, as physicians and pharmaceutical researchers have begun to realize that many of the so-called primitive remedies have remarkable healing qualities and therapeutic value in the

treatment of numerous diseases and conditions, such as cancer, arthritis, heart disease, and high blood pressure.

buster *noun*
See BABY BUSTER.

bust fresh *verb*
(*Slang*) To dress with great style, as in, "Man, she bust fresh out of sight today." An urban street term.

busting *noun*
Mockery of someone, especially through imitation, caricature, or by making fun of their pretensions.

buzz crusher *noun*
(*Slang*) A person who doesn't go along with a good time; party pooper; killjoy.

cable-access programming *noun*
See COMMUNITY-ACCESS PROGRAMMING.

cabotage *noun*
A practice in the airline industry of allowing carriers of one country to carry passengers from one destination to another within a second country. For example, if Japan Air Lines, on a New York–Tokyo trip, picks up a passenger in New York and leaves the passenger off in Seattle, this constitutes cabotage.

Caller ID *noun*
A new telephone service that allows the recipient of a phone call to identify the calling party by displaying the caller's phone number on a liquid crystal display screen contained in a small box attached to the telephone. The Caller ID feature is banned in several states and the subject of controversy in others, mainly over the issue of the rights of privacy of the calling party, who may wish to remain anonymous. Also called **Caller Identification.** See BLOCKING.

campus rape *noun*
A rape that takes place at a college campus or dormitory or at a college-related facility, such as a fraternity or sorority house.

can bank *noun*
A machine or bin, typically located at a supermarket, in which consumers can deposit empty cans for recycling.

canned hunt *noun*
The illegal practice of shooting captured, caged, or disabled game animals, frequently at point-blank range. According to *Time* magazine, a videotape of one such hunt "shows the leopard being released from a cage and running under a nearby pickup truck. A pack of dogs flushed it out of hiding, and for $3,000, a 'hunter' from Louisiana had the privilege of shooting the panic stricken animal."

Caprenin (ka-PREE-nin) *noun*
A fat substitute, manufactured by Proctor and Gamble, that is composed of a variety of fatty acids and has only about half the calories of other fats. See FAT SUBSTITUTE.

carboplatin (CAR-bo-platt-in) *noun*
A new drug used to treat testicular cancer.

car clout *noun*
A car break-in, as in a parking lot of a national park. "A rash of car clouts, as the break-ins are called, occurred last year, according to Marsh Karle, assistant public affairs officer at Yosemite." (*New York Times*)

cardiomyoplasty (car-dee-o-MY-o-plas-tee) *noun*
A surgical procedure in which damaged heart tissue is replaced with muscle tissue from the patient's back.

Cardiopump *noun*
A new medical device developed by researchers at the University of California at San Francisco that seems to work better than traditional CPR (cardiopulmonary resuscitation). "The Cardiopump," explains *New York Times* science writer Lawrence K. Altman, "is placed on a victim's bare chest. Gripping the device with both hands, much as in using a steering wheel, the rescuer pushes and pulls on it the same 80 times a minute as in standard CPR. With the new device performing both compression and decompression actively, more blood is pumped through the coronary arteries than with CPR. It has the further advantage of drawing air into the lungs."

Carhenge *noun*
A full-size replica of Stonehenge built entirely of junked cars instead of stone. It is located in Alliance, Nebraska, and has become a popular tourist attraction.

catastrophic care *noun*
A health insurance coverage category designating a major, congenital, or chronic condition or illness, ranging from

Down syndrome to paralysis to vegetative coma, and being typically of a nature that exhausts the financial resources of the patient and the patient's family. Federal insurance funds have increasingly been drained by the costs of hospital, at-home, or nursing home care. According to an editorial in the *Boston Globe*, "The Catastrophic Health Act of 1989 which broadened Medicare coverage was quickly repealed. Brave promises by members of Congress to restore the extended coverage — and to more evenly finance it — have turned to dust." Also called **catastrophe health insurance.**

catazine *noun*
See MAGALOG.

CD-I (SEE-dee-EYE) *noun*
An interactive compact disk product or technology. CD-I combines computer power with compact disk storage technology to allow the user to create or respond to complex images and sounds produced on state-of-the-art video or audio equipment.

CD + G *noun*
Compact disk plus graphics. See CD TV.

CD TV *noun*
A combination of compact disk, audio, television, and microcomputer technology that allows the user to select and combine visual and auditory sources to create educational and entertainment experiences. For example, the user can browse through an electronic encyclopedia to find a selection on Mozart and then, by pressing a button, can hear selections from one of Mozart's symphonies.

ceiling test *noun*
An accounting term in the natural gas industry that refers to an SEC rule requiring an adjustment to earnings, called

the **ceiling write-down,** that realistically reflects the recoverable value of assets. The ceiling test, according to accounting specialist Rick Corn, "is designed to keep book values for energy reserves from ranging too high compared with revenues and earnings. It gives investors an idea of how much net revenue a company would generate if its reserves were produced until no longer feasible at a given price."

cerebrally challenged *adjective*
Slow-learning. A bias-free term.

Ceredase (SEHR-uh-days) *noun*
A trademark for a new drug for treating Gaucher's disease type 1, a rare, debilitating genetic disorder most common among Ashkenazi Jews. The modified form of a natural human enzyme, developed and manufactured by Genzyme Corp., Ceredase was approved by the Food and Drug Administration in April 1991. According to *The Jewish Week*, it "not only halts the illness, but over time, reverses it."

CFS *noun*
See CHRONIC FATIGUE SYNDROME.

CFTC
Abbreviation of Commodity Futures Trading Commission.

Chabad (huh-BAHD) *noun*
A name for the Lubavitch movement, a sect of ultra-orthodox Jews based in Brooklyn, New York, and Israel who believe in the imminent arrival of the Messiah.

Channel One *noun*
A satellite-delivered morning news program featuring news anchors who are 18 to 24 years of age. The program

is broadcast to middle and high schools during the school day and is designed to be used as a teaching tool. Each program, twelve minutes in length, has commercial time of two minutes broken into four 30-second spots. Whittle Communications provides this closed-circuit program free to the schools in exchange for the rights to sell the commercial time.

channel surf *verb*
To change television channels with a remote control in an idle search for entertainment. "Channel-surfing late one night I happened upon Sandra's HBO special. It was specially awful, even by late-night TV standards." (Diane White, *Boston Globe*)

chat system *noun*
An online electronic bulletin board service, such as Compuserve, that allows interactive participation and computer conferencing.

cheat sheet *noun*
A template placed above, on the side of, or around a computer keyboard that shows the codes needed to run a particular program. The cheat sheet is especially useful where the commands are not intuitive: where, for instance, *S* is not for *Save* and *P* is not for *Print*.

Checkout Channel *noun*
A video channel featuring news shorts and features designed for the shopper waiting in a checkout line. Installed in a number of supermarkets throughout the US, this Turner Broadcasting subsidiary carries the commercials of advertisers whose products are on the store shelves.

Cheese *noun*
Ironic treatment of popular entertainment of a previous time, as the 1950s, that mocks its quality of kitsch without

having camp's attitude of affectionate celebration. "Cheese, a more mean-spirited, mocking esthetic. Whereas Camp is someone trying to impersonate Marilyn Monroe or Judy Garland out of a sense of identification, Cheese is someone imitating Donny Osmond or Barry Manilow out of a sense of satire and contempt." (Michiko Kakutani, *New York Times*)

Chicago pizza *noun*
A thick-crusted pizza that is "stuffed, as opposed to topped, with a variety of robust combinations (some have goofy names) and served in a deep pan." (*New York Magazine*) [From *Chicago*, Illinois, where it originated in a restaurant called Uno's.]

chill hard *verb*
(*Slang*) **1.** To hang out; socialize, with the implication of the use of drugs. **2.** To stay cool; relax; get with it. Originally an urban street term, it has become part of the language of rap music and entered the mainstream through advertising geared to a young urban market.

Chinese wall *noun*
A protective strategy used by fund managers, institutional investors, and cautious banking and investment firms, that, according to finance writer Diana B. Henriques, comprises "a combination of physical and procedural barriers to insure that their investment bankers don't share private client information with the firm's traders, who could profit from the inside knowledge." Enforcement usually requires that the signer pledge not to trade in certain securities, or groups of securities, to which he or she has privileged information, known commonly as the **Chinese wall letter.**

chlorine monoxide *noun*
An ozone-depleting chemical byproduct of the chlorofluorocarbons, responsible for weakening the earth's protective shield and contributing to the greenhouse effect.

chop *noun*
See TOMAHAWK CHOP.

chronic fatigue syndrome *noun*
A disorder of unknown, possibly viral origin that is characterized by lethargy, muscle pain, mild depression, low-grade fever, loss of energy, and other symptoms and is sometimes mistaken for hypochondria. Also called **CFS; Iceland disease; Royal Free disease.**

Chunnel *noun*
A name (a blend of *Ch*annel and *tunnel*) for the tunnel beneath the English Channel that is expected to link England and France by the mid 1990s.

circuit breaker *noun*
A securities market and futures-trading mechanism in which an automatic suspension of trading occurs under certain predefined conditions indicative of unstable or wildly vacillating markets. For example, a stock's trading may be automatically suspended through a circuit breaker when its trading reaches 150% of normal within a two-hour period.

CIS *noun*
A federation of self-governing states formed in 1991 and including most of the republics of the former Soviet Union. [Abbreviation of Commonwealth of Independent States]

clacker *noun*
See KLICKSTICK.

classism *noun*
Oppression of the working class and nonpropertied by the upper and middle classes.

climbing gym *noun*
A health club facility that offers indoor sport climbing. See SPORT CLIMBING.

climbing wall *noun*
See SPORT CLIMBING.

closed adoption *noun*
An adoption of an infant in which the birth parents and adoptive parents do not meet and receive a minimal amount of information about each other, making the identification of the birth parents difficult later in life for the adopted child.

clothesline *verb*
In football, to grab an opposing player illegally by encircling his neck with an arm.

club class *noun*
Business class seating, as designated by some airlines.

club-pack products *noun*
A supermarket retailing concept, developed in response to the growing competition of food clubs, that involves selling common products in bulk, such as 12-roll bundles of toilet paper and 24-can cases of soft drinks, to keep the prices down and the products moving in sufficient volume.

clutch-hitting index *noun*
A baseball statistic that measures various aspects of a batter's ability to perform well with men on base, and combines these, through a mathematical formula, into a single numerical indicator. "At the root of the index," according to its developers, John Thorn and Pete Palmer, "is a study done by Mr. Palmer that determined the average contribution of every kind of baseball event to the scoring of a

run. . . . The clutch-hitting index divides the number of a player's actual runs batted in (r.b.i.) in a season by a figure called 'expected r.b.i.' " (*New York Times*)

clydesdale *noun*
(*Slang*) A good-looking young man who is dating an equally attractive young woman.

CMO *noun*
A financial instrument in which federal mortgage–backed bonds are grouped together as an investment security. [Abbreviation of Collateralized Mortgage Obligation]

COBE (кон-bee) *noun*
Acronym for **C**osmic **B**ackground **E**xplorer, a satellite that is an integral part of NASA's effort to discover the origins of the universe by monitoring minuscule amounts of background microwave radiation in outer space.

coca puff *noun*
(*Slang*) A marijuana cigarette laced with cocaine.

codec *noun*
A device used to transmit video images over ordinary phone lines for video conferencing. [From *coder-dec*oder]

coercive potential *noun*
The capability of bombs to harm and demoralize soldiers, as opposed to the measurement of number of deaths and extent of property damage. A military buzzword.

cohousing *noun*
A communal-based housing concept, originating in Denmark but made popular in the US by architect Charles Durrett, that has been enjoying increasing popularity in recent

years. Cohousing is the process whereby the potential residents of a housing community do the designing and building themselves, with close attention to community needs, interests, and limitations, especially those of a financial nature. It combines some elements of condominium ownership and of limited partnership development practices. Decisions governing a variety of stages from land acquisition to financing and construction to management after tenancy are made by committee.

cold chillin' *noun*
(*Slang*) A good time.

cold dark matter *noun*
A hypothetical material consisting of subatomic particles that, according to some cosmological theories, was produced at the beginning of time and comprises up to 90 percent of all the matter in the universe. Also called **dark matter.**

cold fusion *noun*
The still unproven theoretical process of creating energy-releasing nuclear fusion, normally occurring only at extremely high temperatures, at or near room temperature. Widely publicized claims to have achieved cold fusion in a University of Utah laboratory in early 1990 were discredited by the scientific community two years later.

collective engagement *noun*
The Western nations' post–cold war foreign policy, combining consideration of the environment, health, humanitarianism, economic development, security, and military needs into international cooperative efforts. Norway's Prime Minister Gro Harlem Brundtland, speaking at Harvard University's 1992 commencement exercises, said,

"The West has won the Cold War. Now the West must again resume real leadership. We need a collective engagement which goes beyond building a new East–West relationship. We need a new era of internationalism where peace, environment and development are linked, placed in the epicenter of national and international affairs."

color healing *noun*
   An experimental form of holistic therapy that attempts to affect a patient's physical responses by shining colored lights on the body to alter its "vibrations," or "aura."

comfort women *noun plural*
   Korean women who were forced by the Japanese to work as prostitutes in brothels during World War II. Now politically organized, these women have protested visits by Japanese leaders and other activities between the Korean and Japanese governments that attempt to improve relations between the two countries. Also called **inanfu; comfort girls.**

comfort zone *noun*
   The context of living and working conditions that one is used to, including habits and patterns of living and behavior. Robert J. Eaton of the Chrysler Corporation recently said, in discussing what it will take to make the new generation of cars succeed, "We need to operate outside our comfort zone to make this thing work."

communicoding *noun*
   A process of communication between right-brained and left-brained thinkers, whose thinking is either linear-oriented or conceptually oriented, so as to bridge the gap between them through clear language and precise examples.

communitarian *noun*
   A believer in communitarianism. A communitarian would typically be against the strict requirements for search

and seizure and in favor of laws that allow police to pick people up for loitering and vagrancy, a common police strategy used to fight street corner drug dealers.

communitarianism *noun*
The belief that the rights of individuals have expanded so much that the rights of the community as a whole are jeopardized.

community-access programming *noun*
Local television programs, often of amateur quality, aired on cable channels under a federal law that allows free, noncommercial air time to any person or group that requests it. The popular *Saturday Night Live* sketch "Wayne's World," which became a hugely successful 1991 film, is a spoof of the worst aspects of community-access programming. Also called **cable-access programming.**

commuter mug *noun*
A plastic beverage mug designed especially for commuters. The mug has a removable water-tight lid with a sipping hole in it through which the commuter can drink hot or cold liquids without fear of spilling. Some models come with holders that adhere to a car's dashboard.

companion animal *noun*
See ANIMAL COMPANION.

compassionate fare *noun*
A significantly reduced airline fare made available to people who are traveling to attend a funeral or visit someone very ill. To qualify for this fare, a customer must document the emergency or compassionate nature of the travel need and establish his or her relationship to the deceased or ill person. Also called **bereavement fare.**

compound Q *noun*
A promising cancer-treatment drug that is an extract from Chinese cucumber root. One form of it, GLQ223, is licensed for experimental use in the United States. [Q perhaps from *cucumber*] Also called **trichosanthin.**

compulsory license *noun*
A rule in federal broadcasting that permits any cable system to carry all over-the-air TV stations in its geographical region without having to pay any fees.

computer book *noun*
See PAPERLESS BOOK.

condom earring *noun*
An earring that looks like a rolled condom and is used to promote the importance of safe sex by encouraging people to speak about condoms without embarrassment. Condom earrings are sold under the brand name **Safe Ears.**

cond-op *noun*
A hybrid between a condominium and a co-op, useful in conforming with a variety of IRS regulations that place limitations on either form by itself. The designation of cond-op allows a residential building to lease out commercial space on the ground floor, as part of a condominium structure, while the upper residential floors comprise their own co-op.

Condor *noun*
A pilotless experimental aircraft developed by the Boeing Corporation and designed to cruise for days or weeks at a time, soaring to altitudes far above those possible for crewed aircraft and for distances as far as 20,000 miles without refueling. See ENDOSAT.

connection machine *noun*
A supercomputer that uses massively parallel processing to achieve extremely high-speed calculation results. See MASSIVELY PARALLEL PROCESSING.

conscious connected breathing *noun*
See REBIRTHING.

consensual non-monogamy *noun*
A practice in which pairs of marital partners temporarily switch mates for sex. Formerly known as *swinging* or *swapping*.

content testing *noun*
The practice in Hollywood filmmaking of testing audience reaction to a film immediately before its final editing in order to reach decisions, especially about the film's ending, that may affect its commercial success. "Many directors denounce the practice, fearing the effects of market research on creative art. But others embrace [content] testing as a tool for honing their work." (Neal Koch, *New York Times*)

contingent worker *noun*
A person who is part of the contingent work force. According to Robert Lewis, "contingent workers now hold one in four jobs in America — a total of about 30 million."

contingent work force *noun*
The work force performing part-time, temporary, work-for-hire, or freelance work on a regular basis in order to supplement a full-time income, to provide additional income during retirement, or because it is the only work available.

control slip *noun*
A woman's lightweight undergarment that combines the features of a girdle and a slip and helps shape the body without the constraining force of the old-fashioned garments.

cool pose *noun*
A defiant swagger and bold posturing identified with inner-city Black youths. Psychologist Dr. Richard Majors, who has written a book on the subject, sees the cool pose as helping a person to "maintain a sense of integrity and suppress rage at being blocked from usual routes to esteem and success." (*New York Times*)

copayment *noun*
A health coinsurance payment in which a total approved charge is paid jointly on a predetermined percentage basis by different parties, as by the patient and the insurance company or by the primary insurer and major medical insurer.

copreneur *noun*
A couple who establish and operate their own business, usually under a partnership arrangement. [From *couple* + entre*preneur*]

copreneurship (koh-pruh-NER-ship, koh-pruh-NOOR-ship) *noun*
The practice of running a business as copreneurs, a rapidly growing phenomenon in an unstable business economy. Copreneurship is the focus of a new organization called the National Association of Entrepreneurial Couples (Eugene, Oregon), founded by husband and wife team Frank and Haran Barnett.

coral bleaching *noun*
The destruction of coral reefs through unsound environmental practices, such as unregulated sewage disposal, or natural phenomena, such as the warm ocean current El Niño. Also called **bleaching.**

court-in *noun*
An initiation ceremony among female gang members, especially in the inner city of Los Angeles. The initiation consists of a 13-second beating of the new member by other gang members. "At the court-in, a girl is christened with the nickname by which she will be known and, as one former gang member put it, suddenly finds that there are 30 or 40 people ready to die for her." (*New York Times*)

cram school *noun*
See JUKU.

crash TV *noun*
Television programming in which the excitement of video games serves as the model for a TV show. Crash TV shows range from "RollerGames" to "Super Mario Brothers" cartoons.

crispy *adjective*
(*Slang*) Suffering from a hangover, as in, "He's feeling crispy this morning after last night's bash."

Croatia (kroh-AY-shuh) *noun*
A former republic of Yugoslavia that declared its independence in June 1991. The capital is Zagreb.

crowd swim *verb*
To make one's way through a dense crowd, as at a concert or on a dance floor, by ducking under, easing around,

or gliding gracefully through the narrow spaces between people.

cruelty-free *adjective*
Of, relating to, or being a food or product that has not, at any stage of development, exposed animals to laboratory testing or harsh circumstances. For example, veal is not regarded as being cruelty-free because the calves are force-fed milk, and only free-range chickens are held to be cruelty-free. The term is used especially by vegetarians and animal rights advocates.

crufty *adjective*
(Of a software program or operating system) Poorly constructed or clumsy. Used especially by computer hackers.

crunch time *noun*
The critical time in a basketball game when a team must make a maximum effort to come from behind or hold on to its lead.

crunchy granola *noun*
A person who is emotionally or temperamentally still living in the 1960s, as expressed in dress, language, or social values.

crystal healing *noun*
A form of New Age therapy that alleges to provide healing energy from quartz or other crystals.

crystal meth *noun*
See ICE.

cultural genocide *noun*
Any philosophy, policy, or practice that is seen to oppress chiefly minority groups directly or indirectly. Accusations

of cultural genocide have been made against school systems that attempt to teach English to Hispanic students and against world health agencies that bring infant formula to poor countries. A bias-free term.

cultural jammer *noun*
An artist who satirizes the mass media and its corporate sponsorship by means of music, billboards, and other forms. Using the common icons and language of the mass media, the cultural jammers combine advertising slogans and jingles with the banalities of old television shows to produce an art of protest. Also called **jammer.** See OUTSIDER ART; TERRORIST ART.

cyberspace (SY-ber-spays) *noun*
See ARTIFICIAL REALITY.

Czech and Slovak Federal Republic *noun*
The name created in June 1992 for the former communist country of Czechoslovakia. By agreement of Czech and Slovak leaders, the country is scheduled to be divided into two sovereign states in 1993.

D

daily value *noun*
A new and expanded category used to replace the older, less inclusive term "Recommended Daily Allowance" in referring to suggested human intake of nutrients, includ-

ing vitamins, minerals, fats, fibers, sodium, and calories. See DV.

dancecore *noun*
See INDUSTRIAL DISCO.

Danforth *verb*
To advise (a patient) at the time of admission to a hospital of his or her right to refuse life-sustaining measures if the need should arise, as in, "Has that patient been Danforthed?" [Named after Missouri Senator John Danforth, who cosponsored the law that made such an advisory mandatory as of December 1991]

dango *noun*
A bid-rigging practice in Japan in which an organized group of large construction companies, known as the **dango cartel,** consult in secret before submitting bids. These companies not only decide among themselves who will submit the winning bid, but also agree on how much of the total business will be parceled out to the other participants, who serve as subcontractors.

dark matter *noun*
See COLD DARK MATTER.

DCC *noun*
A new recording medium that uses digital technology for recording and playback and is incompatible with traditional analog cassette recording technology. [Abbreviation of Digital Compact Cassette] Also called **digital compact cassette.**

DDC *noun*
An antiviral medication, **dideoxycytidine,** that is being tested experimentally in the treatment of AIDS.

DDE *noun*

The exchange of information among different computer programs, a rapidly growing trend among computer software developers and hardware manufacturers. With DDE, for example, a spreadsheet written in Lotus 1-2-3 can easily share information, such as data and formulas, with an entirely different document prepared with any word processing program, database, or even a presentation graphics program. [Abbreviation of Dynamic Data Exchange] Also called **dynamic data exchange**. See OLE.

DDI *noun*

An experimental drug developed by Bristol-Myers Squibb for use in the treatment of AIDS, especially as an alternative for patients who show intolerance for the more commonly used AZT. Also called **didanosine**.

dead-cat bounce *noun*

A false sign of market recovery. "This applies to stocks or commodities that have gone into freefall descent and then rallied briefly. If you threw a dead cat off a 50-story building, it might bounce when it hit the sidewalk. But don't confuse the bounce with renewed life. It is still a dead cat." (Raymond DeVoe, Jr.)

Dead dancing *noun*

A kind of wobbly, free-flowing, spontaneous audience dancing that originated at The Grateful Dead concerts in the 1960s and has maintained vitality along with that aging but still popular rock group.

Deadhead *noun*

An ardent follower of the rock band The Grateful Dead.

deadtime *noun*

(In environmental science) The time it takes an item to biodegrade into an organic, bacteria-digestible form.

deathbelt *noun*
   Alabama, Texas, Mississippi, and Arkansas, together having the highest execution rates in the nation. A term used by death penalty opponents.

decadize *verb*
   To categorize into a decade historical trends and events that, in fact, straddle a period of time touching different decades. For example, what is generally called the 60s typically includes events and trends stretching from 1963–64 to about 1973.

dedicated tax *noun*
   A tax that, by law, may only be put to certain specific uses. For example, taxes on gasoline may only be used for highway and transportation programs, and lottery taxes (revenues) are geared toward educational programs. The current move toward dedicated taxes includes proposals to dedicate new cigarette and liquor taxes to offsetting the enormous health care expenses incurred by smokers and drinkers. The philosophy behind these taxes is that citizens will be more willing to pay them if their money is specifically earmarked for programs they need or approve of.

deep doo-doo *noun*
   (*Slang*) Serious trouble. [A precious allusion to feces]

defensin *noun*
   Any of a class of antibiotics made by immune cells called neutrophils. These natural protein compounds can destroy microbes by piercing their membranes, according to Natalie Angier of the *New York Times*. "Essentially, they make the bacteria very leaky. And any time you make a cell leaky, that cell is going to die." (Dr. Michael E. Seisted)

Delphi method *noun*
A management technique in which employee or lower management decision-making takes place through small groups in which individual members can make candid comments that they might be reluctant to make directly to supervisors.

demarketing *noun*
Social marketing that attempts to bring about a loss of interest in things viewed by many as negative and dangerous, such as smoking or the use of nuclear power. See SOCIAL MARKETING.

denied-boarding compensation *noun*
An airline compensation payment made in cash or in travel vouchers to passengers who have been bumped from a flight on which they had reservations.

depantsing *noun*
See SCUTTLING.

deuce-five *noun*
(*Slang*) A .25 caliber handgun.

didanosine (dy-DAN-uh-sin) *noun*
See DDI.

dideoxycytidine (dy-dee-ok-see-SY-ti-deen) *noun*
See DDC.

differently abled *adjective*
Handicapped; disabled. A bias-free term.

digerati (dij-ur-RAH-tee) *noun*
People who are highly skilled in the processing and manipulation of digital information. [Modeled on *literati*]

digital broadcasting *noun*

A new television technology, designed to supersede traditional analog broadcasting, in which signals are sent as strings of binary numbers (0s and 1s), providing significantly less distortion (noise), flutter, and other environmental and transmission disturbances. Digital television broadcasting also allows greater manipulation of the transmission source: visual frames can be frozen or enhanced, small sections of a picture can be boxed within larger sections, and sounds can be cleaned up and made more resonant. The technology can also be used for radio broadcasting, where it is known alternatively as **digital radio** or **digital audio broadcasting.**

digital compact cassette *noun*

See DCC.

digital compression *noun*

A computer technology in which a large amount of digital information in binary form (0s and 1s) is compressed into a smaller space. The information may consist of audio sounds, broadcast programs, graphics, photographic information, or plain text; the space may be on a computer's disk, over the air on a broadcasting channel, or in any other suitable medium. The compression is achieved through a sequence of formulas that eliminate white space (blank areas, such as the borders on a page) and code redundant elements, such as repeating letters, punctuation, and repeated sounds.

digital photography *noun*

A still image photography technique combining the technologies of computers, video electronics, and photography. A recording unit, sometimes called a **filmless camera,** that is approximately the size of a 35-millimeter camera, encodes the visual information into digital form, allowing the picture to be recorded and stored on a magnetic disk that can be played back on a regular television set. By storing information in digital form, a photographer can also make modifications in the recorded image. Also called **electronic still video; filmless photography.**

digital radio *noun*
See DIGITAL BROADCASTING.

digital sampler *noun*
A computerized musical device in which a computer reprocesses brief digitized fragments of instrumental and voice information (such as a Jimi Hendrix guitar riff or a bar from a Van Morrison song) to create a full range of sounds that can be altered, combined, synthesized, or expanded (*stretched*) by the performer or composer creating a new work. "Unlike synthesizers, which generate tones artificially, [digital] samplers record real sounds . . . they transform these sounds into digital codes, which in turn can be manipulated to produce melodies, rhythm tracks, and complicated webs of sounds." (*Time*) The process is called **digital sampling.**

diplolingo (DIP-lo-ling-go) *noun*
The language of international media circles. [Coined by William Safire of the *New York Times*]

diss *verb*
(*Slang*) To treat disrespectfully; insult; snap. An urban street term.

distance education *noun*
New educational strategies and technologies that link together in an interactive network teachers and students in

distant places through the instantaneous information transmission capabilities of satellites, optical fiber, copper wire, or microwave telecommunication technology. By creating what are called **virtual classrooms,** students and teachers in remote areas of the world can interact with each other, using computers, video monitors, and telephone equipment in simultaneous course work that would otherwise be unavailable to them. See AG*SAT; LEARNING CIRCLES.

DNR *noun*

A code indicating to health care personnel that extraordinary life-sustaining procedures should not be used on a patient. [Abbreviation of Do Not Resuscitate]

doggin' *noun*

(*Teenage Slang*) Cheating on one's partner.

dolo *adverb*

(*Slang*) On one's own; alone; solo.

Dolphin Safe *adjective*

Of, relating to, or being tuna caught with nets that do not endanger or accidently snare dolphins. According to James Brooke, in the *New York Times,* "A ship's tuna catch is rated 'Dolphin Safe' under American consumer law only if an international onboard observer certifies that no dolphins were killed during the netting operations."

dolphin think *noun*

A technique for maximizing business power by cunningly outmaneuvering one's larger and more formidable opponents and competitors.

domestic partnership *noun*

A publicly recognized although not legally sanctioned marriagelike partnership between lesbian or gay male partners. Some municipalities, such as New York City, Minneapolis, and San Francisco, have allowed these long-term domestic partnerships to be officially recorded and acknowledged for purposes of health and life insurance, compassionate release time, and survivor's benefits.

domo *noun*
A downwardly mobile professional, typically a person under 40 who abandons a successful or promising career to concentrate on more meaningful or spiritual activities. [From *do*wnwardly *mo*bile]

do-not-call database *noun*
A proposed national database of people who do not wish to be solicited by telemarketers, according to *DM News*. Widely debated by legislators and the FCC, several different versions of this database have been proposed, ranging from a computerized file that would be made available to all telemarketers, to the use of asterisks preceding names in telephone directories. Each has drawn many objections and none has succeeded in gaining wide favor. Still, as increasing numbers of telephone subscribers complain about the annoyance of these unsolicited calls, new solutions for this problem are being sought.

doomsday rock *noun*
See EARTH-CROSSING ASTEROID.

dope *verb*
(*Slang*) To treat deceitfully or insincerely, as in the expression, "You doping me about this?" An urban street term.

dope on a rope *adjective*
(*Teenage Slang*) Really great; cool. (Jeanne Jackson, *Asbury Park Press*)

DOS extender (dos) *noun*

A computer program that allows the limited memory range of the DOS operating system to expand considerably by tricking the computer into accepting programs that are actually above the 640k limit of the machine. Also called **extender**. See PROTECTED MODE; VIRTUAL-86 MODE.

double dip recession *noun*

An economic concept describing a three-part related sequence of recession, a brief recovery, and a subsequent recession, all linked together by a nexus of hidden economic forces.

downtown *noun*

A magazine market segment consisting of a highly influential readership. Magazines for this small, vaguely defined, and trend-setting market segment, usually in the Washington, DC, Los Angeles, Boston, or New York City regions, compete with each other for a limited number of subscribers.

downtown improvisation *noun*

A semi-improvisational music that combines elements of jazz, modern-classical, and minimalism and is often performed in underground clubs and small concert halls.

down with *adjective*

(*Teenage Slang*) Being intimate with or part of, as in, "I'm down with that crowd."

dowry death *noun*

The murder in India of a new bride, committed because her family does not contribute a sufficient dowry to the marriage. Many such murders have been recorded in India, where the Hindu system of dowries is entrenched. A term used primarily by women's rights organizations in India.

Dow Text *noun*
A proprietary typeface design, owned by Dow Jones & Company, recently redesigned for use in *The Wall Street Journal*, a Dow Jones publication.

dpi *noun*
A measurement used to determine the density and clarity of print produced by computer printers that form their text and images using configurations of small dots. An inexpensive impact printer may have 81 dpi, while a typical laser printer will use 300 dots per inch. [Abbreviation of Dots Per Inch]

drink box *noun*
A small, rectangular, airtight juice container that has a self-contained straw, requires no refrigeration, and fits snugly into a lunch box. The drink box's aseptic package consists of alternating layers of polyethylene plastic, aluminum foil, and paper, providing an air-resistant and water-resistant barrier that protects the juice from contamination, leakage, oxidation, and spoilage. Also called **juice box.**

drop-in center *noun*
A community-based social services facility that requires no appointment, often used in working with people who are homeless, substance addicted, abused, or in crisis.

drug war *noun*
The government's local, regional, national, and international efforts to combat drug production, distribution, and sales. The term generally includes the combined use of in-

telligence and military forces, guided by national policies and specialized laws and treaties.

drum machine *noun*
An electronic instrument that consists of a flat surface, a computerized sound generator, and specially constructed drum sticks and generates percussive sounds through amplification and digital sampling. See SAMPLING.

ductless split *noun*
An air-conditioning technology in which the noisy components, such as the motor, are outside the room and the refrigerant and fans are inside.

dudical (DOO-di-kuhl) *noun*
(*Teenage Slang*) A person whose unconventional ideas and behavior sets him or her apart from the general populace. Also called **radical dude.**

dumbth *noun*
The contemporary American's purported ignorance in significant categories of knowledge, such as the environment, politics, international relations, finance, and the arts. [Coined by Steve Allen, it is also the title of his 1991 book *DUMBTH: And 81 Ways to Make Americans Smarter*]

duopoly *noun*
A situation in broadcasting in which a single company owns more than one AM or FM station in a given market. [From *du*al + mon*opoly*]

DV *noun*
The FDA's new designation for the suggested nutritional needs quotas listed on food labels. [Abbreviation of Daily Value] See DAILY VALUE.

DVI *noun*

A CD-I technology offering three-dimensional modeling. [Abbreviation of Digital Video Interactive] See CD-I.

DWEM *noun*

A Caucasian male historical figure, such as Plato, Shakespeare, Leonardo, Mozart, Einstein, or Henry James, who by tradition dominates the study of Western culture. Used pejoratively by some political activists. [Acronym for **D**ead **W**hite **E**uropean **M**ale]

dynamic data exchange *noun*

See DDE.

dyslipidemia (DISS-lip-id-EEM-ee-uh) *noun*

A disorder characterized by excessive fatlike substances in the blood and involving high cholesterol levels.

E

earth-crossing asteroid *noun*

Any asteroid whose orbit might at some future time intersect that of Earth. There are about 150 such asteroids that have been identified, and new ones are being sighted each month. Some of the larger asteroids are several miles wide and pose catastrophic danger in the event of a crash. Also called **doomsday rock**. See KILLER ASTEROID.

Earthship *noun*

A dwelling originated by New Mexico architect Michael Reynolds and built mainly of used and dirt-packed tires, aluminum cans, and other recycled materials. An Earthship is said to be energy-efficient and environmentally sound, as well as relatively cheap to build.

Earth Summit *noun*
A conference held in Rio de Janeiro, Brazil, in June 1992 to discuss the environmental issues facing all the nations of the world.

Easy Reach 700 *noun*
A new telephone service by which a subscriber is assigned a permanent long-distance number that begins with the area code 700. Unlike ordinary area codes, the 700 number does not identify a particular region but rather remains with the individual for as long as he or she wishes and wherever he or she resides. Also called **lifetime telephone number; portable telephone number.**

EBITDA (ee-bit-DEE-ay)
Abbreviation for the accounting phrase Earnings Before Interest, Taxes, Depreciation, and Amortization.

eco-babble *noun*
Proposals, theories, and ideas considered nonsense from a scientific point of view by environmental scientists.

eco-justice *noun*
The concept, now much debated in theological circles, that the protection of the environment is an integral part of a greater God-willed mission of humankind.

eco-office *noun*
An office that has been designed to be environmentally free of indoor pollution and other contaminants. See SICK BUILDING SYNDROME.

eco-pak *noun*

A recyclable cardboard package designed to hold compact disks and to replace the nonrecyclable plastic **jewel box** largely in current use. During the past two years most major record labels have agreed to phase in the use of eco-paks.

eco-ranching *noun*

A type of ranching that by considering the ecological implications of all business decisions, is conservationally sound and environmentally sensitive. Eco-ranching tries to combine effective production methods with natural resource replenishment. See NEW CONSERVATION.

ecotourism *noun*

Nature-oriented travel, generally to pristine, natural, or little-explored areas. Increasingly popular with environmentally and ecologically aware tourists, ecotourism combines many of the benefits of educational travel with the quiet pleasures of relaxation, free from the traditional hectic pace of tourism.

Ecowriter *noun*

See AMERICAN ECOWRITER.

ecstasy *noun*

A mind-altering drug, technically MDMA for 3,4 methylene dioxymethamphetamine, that is derived from the amphetamines and is said to produce feelings of well-being, heightened alertness, and generalized benevolence. It was declared an illegal drug in 1985 as having no medical usefulness and a high potential for abuse.

edge city *noun*

An area of high commercial and residential density that is at the nexus of transportation systems and highways. An edge city displays a high density of malls, retail shops, office buildings, convention centers, and hotels. A byproduct of declining downtowns and decaying suburbs, edge cities, themselves neither city nor suburb, seemed to burst forth spontaneously as cheaper land was acquired and developed within a fifty-mile radius of a population or business hub. [Coined by author Joel Garreau]

EDLP *noun*

A new marketing policy that promises lower prices to the consumer at retail on a simplified regular basis, without sales, discounting, or promotional events. This is usually accomplished, as Julie Liesse of *Advertising Age* reported, "with the concept of cutting or adjusting trade promotion programs in favor of lower list prices to retailers." [Abbreviation of Everyday Low Pricing] Also called **everyday low pricing.**

E-lamp *noun*

A new long-lasting light bulb that uses high-frequency radio waves to excite a gas mixture inside the bulb instead of heating a metal filament, as in an incandescent bulb. The E-lamp is considerably more energy efficient and less expensive to operate than either the conventional incandescent bulb or the fluorescent bulb. [From Electronic *lamp*] Also called **electronic lamp.**

electric bandage *noun*

A medical device that sends a small electric current through an electrode pad placed on a wound. The application of the painless electrical current of about 30 milliamperes promotes more rapid healing, although the mechanisms of the process remain unknown.

electric slide *noun*

A line dance that originated in clubs in Washington, DC's Black community and has gradually spread to different parts of the country, gaining much popularity because it does not require a partner. Enjoyed by all age groups, the slide follows an easy three step beat, with the dancer moving along the line first to the left, then the right, then forward and back.

electric van *noun*

A battery-powered van, recently introduced by the Chrysler Corporation, with top speed of 65 mph, a range of 100 miles, and an acceleration that can take it from 0 to 60 in 25 seconds.

electrochromic window *noun*

See SMART WINDOW.

electronic book *noun*

See PAPERLESS BOOK.

electronic cadaver *noun*

A computerized simulation system that is used for teaching anatomy to medical students, supplementing the traditional approach of dissecting real cadavers. According to the *New York Times*, there are several advantages to using the electronic cadaver: "On a computer screen, unlike with a cadaver, surgical mistakes can be tried over and over. The systems may also help compensate for cadaver shortages in some areas of the country."

electronic coupon *noun*

A discount coupon that is issued by a supermarket checkout scanner and is based on what a shopper actually buys, unlike a coupon cut out from a newspaper or distributed on a flyer.

electronic lamp *noun*
See E-LAMP.

electronic price tag *noun*
A digitized marker that lists the price of a product, as on a supermarket shelf, and is linked to a central computer that coordinates the marker with the check-out registers.

electronic publishing *noun*
Publishing in which the product is a computer-readable medium, such as magnetic disk, optical disk, or tape. See PAPERLESS BOOK.

electronic still video *noun*
See DIGITAL PHOTOGRAPHY.

electronic town hall *noun*
A participatory concept promoted by former presidential candidate H. Ross Perot, in which the television networks would broadcast one-issue discussion programs and the public would record their opinions by marking computer cards for mailing to regional tabulating centers. "Consensus would be reached," the *New York Times* said, "and the leaders would know what the public wanted."

elevator surfing *noun*
A dangerous sport sometimes engaged in by urban youths and college students and consisting of riding on top of an elevator cab, jumping from one shaft to another, and attempting to land on a second elevator.

Endosat *noun*
An experimental, microwave-powered, pilotless aircraft designed by Endosat Inc. to fly higher and for longer cruise

durations than present crewed aircraft. Used mostly by the military for atmospheric research, the Endosat and its sister plane, the Condor, represent middle ground research vehicles for altitudes between 10 and 20 miles in the area not covered by crewed aircraft and satellites. See CONDOR.

enediyne (EEN-dye-ine) *noun*
A chemical molecule synthesized at the Scripps Research Institute laboratories and the University of California, San Diego. Enediyne mimics an antibiotic made by soil bacteria and acts like a molecular warhead to wipe out cancerous tumors while leaving most normal cells alone.

engagement *noun*
A new foreign strategy for the future, as espoused by politicians of both parties, that seeks to leave behind outdated policies of isolationism and containment.

ENSO *noun*
A climatic phenomenon affecting rainfall patterns throughout the equatorial Pacific region. During ENSO, which usually occurs every three to seven years, a combination of warming ocean water and lower atmospheric pressure may increase the coastal rains of Peru while at the same time drying out the coastal areas of Australia and India. [Acronym for **El Niño–Southern Oscillation**]

enterprise zone *noun*
An area that offers tax incentives to encourage investment, create or expand businesses, and bring employment to blighted neighborhoods. "Think of enterprise zones," economist Stuart Butler says, "as the domestic equivalent of foreign trade zones." Enterprise zones have become a popular subject of debate in recent years as federal, state, and local governments tackle the problems of urban decay

and the reluctance of the business community to put down stakes in declining and minority neighborhoods. Also called **EZ**.

environmental racism *noun*
The practice of allowing exposure of members of minority groups or Third World peoples to the more dangerous environmental contaminants, as through disposal or manufacturing.

environmental science *noun*
Educational divisions, departments, and courses that deal with traditional studies in chemistry, physics, biology, engineering, and life science from the point of view of their impact on the environment. The goals include making US technology environmentally safe, developing new manufacturing methods, and reaching a better understanding of the medical implications of our environment.

Epogen (EE-puh-jen) *noun*
A drug that stimulates the production of red blood cells and has recently been used in the treatment of AIDS-related complications.

EPW *noun*
An enemy soldier captured by US forces. The term first came into use during the Persian Gulf War of 1991. The term *POW* (prisoner of war) has more recently been used to describe a US soldier captured by the enemy. [Abbreviation of Enemy Prisoner of War]

equitize *verb*
To increase the amount of equity in (a deal, company, or other financial venture or investment).

equity gap *noun*
The earnings gap that exists between men and women. "Women of all ages are paid about 72 cents for every dollar that men earn . . . [but the equity gap] widens with age, leaving women age 50 and older with only 64 percent of the wages paid men." (Robert Lewis, *AARP Bulletin*)

E ray *noun*
A hypothetical carcinogenic ray said to come from deep within the earth and permeate solid walls and structures. The possibility of its existence has generally been discredited by much of the scientific community.

ERIS *noun*
An antiballistic defense system designed to separate the booster rocket of a two-stage antimissile device while it is approaching a target so that the main unit will hit the target at high speed. [Acronym for **E**xoatmospheric **R**e-entry Vehicle **I**nterceptor **S**ystem]

Eritrea (ehr-uh-TREE-uh, ehr-uh-TRAY-uh) *noun*
A region of Ethiopia that since May 1991 has claimed independence and will vote for nationhood in a referendum to be held around May 1993. The capital city is Asmara.

erotomonomania *noun*
A psychological condition in which a man believes without realistic cause that women are sexually hungry for him, entertaining sexual fantasies about him, or trying to lure him into a sexual partnership.

Estonia (eh-STOW-nee-uh) *noun*
A former republic of the Soviet Union that is now an independent country.

Euro-body music *noun*
See INDUSTRIAL DISCO.

Eurobranding *noun*
The process of marketing a product throughout Europe using the same packaging and advertising in each country. Eurobranding allows a company to pool marketing and advertising resources and at the same time creates a wider base of brand identification and multinational product loyalty.

Europalia *noun*
A festival held in Belgium every two years celebrating the harvest season. Each festival features the art and products of a different country. [From *Eur*ope and *opalia* (Latin for harvest festival)]

Euroyank *noun*
A member of the generation of US and European managers taking over Europe's entertainment industry and putting together large recording and film conglomerates. "The Euroyanks pride themselves on their ability to infiltrate, to cajole, to surround [and] may ultimately end up with a bigger, more profitable stake than the Sonys and Matsushitas." (Peter Bart in *Variety*)

everyday low pricing *noun*
See EDLP.

expanded memory *noun*
The memory available in computers based on Intel's 386-chips and 486-chips, being above the 640k limitation of DOS but below the 1-megabyte limit of the original personal computers.

extender *noun*
See DOS EXTENDER.

eye-alogue *noun*
A communication technique in which a person focuses directly but in a nonthreatening way on the eyes of the person he or she wants to influence.

EZ *noun*
See ENTERPRISE ZONE

F

························

face time *noun*
Time spent in face-to-face communication with other people, as opposed to time spent online with them in electronic communication. A term used chiefly by computer hackers.

Fantasy Baseball *noun*
See ROTISSERIE LEAGUE.

fat substitute *noun*
Any of a class of new products that are used in foods to replace fats. Often derived from vegetables or entirely synthetic, these substitutes are lower in calories than fats, free of cholesterol, and are said to approximate the taste of real fat. See CAPRENIN.

fat tooth *noun*
A tendency on the part of many Americans to derive an unhealthy part of their daily calorie intake from fats. [By analogy with *sweet tooth*]

fave
(*Slang*) **1.** *adjective* Favorite: "a fave hangout." **2.** *noun* Favorite: "The fave of Jeff Greenfield and Robin MacNeil, among others, is WFAN wildman, Don Imus." (*Variety*)

Fax Mail *noun*
Self-service facsimile machines installed in post offices around the country and operated by credit card.

fax-on-demand *noun*
A service by which a customer can, by using an ordinary telephone keypad, request a fax from a central source connected to an IVR system. See IVR SYSTEM.

Federal Republic of Yugoslavia *noun*
A country made up of Serbia and Montenegro formed in April 1992, after the secession of four former Yugoslavian republics. It has a population of 12 million, compared with its previous 22.5 million. Belgrade remains the capital.

feevee *noun*
Any fee-based broadcasting service distributed to homes, including pay-per-view and subscription television programming.

femtosecond laser *noun*
An advanced laser that oscillates at 200 femtoseconds (millionths of a billionth of a second), allowing submolecular observations beyond the capabilities of ordinary electron microscopes. See AFM; OPTICAL MOLASSES; OPTICAL TWEEZERS; STM.

fentanyl patch (FEN-tuh-nil) *noun*
A transdermal patch that releases fentanyl, a powerful painkilling drug, directly through the skin.

ferrofluid *noun*
A liquid in which tiny magnetic particles are suspended, allowing the fluid to be held in place permanently. Ferrofluids are used for cooling loudspeakers, in pumps, and in computer disk drives.

fiber farm *noun*
A small farm on which trees are grown quickly and while still small are cut up to produce a variety of engineered wood products, including oriented strand boards. See ORIENTED STRAND BOARDS.

fiddle *noun*
A scheme involving financial finagling, especially on the part of leading businesspeople and government officials. A chiefly Irish English term.

fierce *adjective*
Exciting; trendy. A term now popular among affluent urbanites, it originated as street slang.

Fifth Generation project *noun*
The anticipated advanced integrated computer software and hardware design that Japan was to develop and thereby make American computers obsolete but that so far has failed to come to fruition and seems unlikely to do so.

Fifth World country *noun*
A country that is poorer and less developed than even the Third World or Fourth World countries, as designated by the International Monetary Fund.

filmless camera *noun*
See DIGITAL PHOTOGRAPHY.

filmless photography *noun*
See DIGITAL PHOTOGRAPHY.

fin-syn rule *noun*
Any of a set of regulations issued by the Federal Communications Commission governing syndication and licensing of network television programming. [From *Financial Interest & Syndication*]

fizzbo *noun*
An owner of a property who offers it for sale without the help of a professional real estate agent. [From *FSBO, for sale by owner*]

flake *verb*
(*Slang*) To back down in an argument or retreat from a fight. An urban street term.

flame mail *noun*
Vitriolic correspondence sent over a computer network or in some other electronic form.

flash and trash *noun*
Local television news broadcasts that feature an abundance of sex, violence, and the bizarre in order to boost ratings.

flash chip *noun*
See FLASH MEMORY.

flash drive *noun*
A computer disk drive using flash memory.

flash memory *noun*
Computer memory based on a special chip (**flash chip**) that, unlike ordinary memory chips, can store information even when the computer is turned off. Flash chips may, as

the price comes down, serve as a logical replacement for the considerably slower and less efficient hard disk drive.

Flashmora *noun*

A group of Christian Ethiopians who claim to have been forced into conversion from Judaism against their will. Members of this group are often applicants for emigration to Israel, where, if they were traditionally Jewish, they would immediately be accepted.

flatline *verb*

To lose vitality; die. "Has one of Hollywood's hottest romances finally flatlined? Though both their publicists deny it, rumors persist about a fallout between Kiefer Sutherland and Julia Roberts." (*New York Post*)

flatliner *noun*

A person whose EKG response is recorded as a flat line; essentially, a person who is dead. The term, derived from the 1990 film *Flatliners*, is sometimes used metaphorically to describe an idea or product that is inert or moribund, as in, "That new model turned out to be a real *flatliner*, with minimal sales."

flat tax *noun*

A tax plan, proposed by Jerry Brown during his 1992 bid for the Democratic party's presidential nomination, in which all individuals and businesses would pay a flat 13% tax on income from all sources, except Social Security benefits and unemployment. Some standardized deductions, such as mortgage payments and charitable gifts, would still be permitted under this plan.

flesh *noun*

Meat. A usage preferred by many animal rights activists and others sympathetic to their cause who find *meat* a term that deliberately distances humans from animals.

flight capital *noun*
Foreign investment in a politically stable area, typically the US, usually by investors from politically unstable regions. It is designed to allow the investment greater liquidity and less chance of being lost or frozen than if left in the native country's banks.

flightseeing *noun*
Sightseeing done from a small low-flying plane in areas that would be difficult or impossible to reach from land. See HELI-EXPLORING.

Flo Motion *noun*
An aerobic activity in which the participant exercises different muscles by swinging in various trajectories a clear polyurethane sleeve-shaped **Flo Bag** filled with air and water.

fluoxetine (floo-OK-suh-teen) *noun*
The most widely prescribed antidepressant drug in the world today, marketed as Prozac.

flyaway pack *noun*
A complete small-scale electronic broadcasting unit able to transmit via satellite from anywhere in the world and compact enough to be checked aboard a plane.

Flying K *noun*
A downhill speed skiing activity performed on a straight, steep, and narrow slope for greatest momentum. [Short for flying kilometer]

food pyramid *noun*
The new symbolic drawing of a pyramid developed by the US Department of Agriculture to educate the public about

nutrition. It divides foods into five basic groups and recommends their relative usage: (1) bread, cereal, rice, and pasta group, (2) fruit group, (3) vegetable group, (4) meat, poultry, fish, dry beans, eggs, and nuts group, and (5) milk, yogurt, and cheese group. It advises the sparing use of fats, oils, and sweets.

footbag *noun*
A game in which one or more people kick an imitation suede bag around in an effort to keep it off the ground. Also called **Hackey Sack; shreddin'.**

forex *noun*
The trading market for foreign currency. [From *for*eign *ex*change]

fossil *noun*
(*Slang*) A college student who has been on campus for a much longer time than might be expected.

Four Tigers *noun*
The four major Asian exporting nations that, along with Japan, contribute most significantly to the US trade deficit because of their efficient manufacturing methods: Hong Kong, Singapore, South Korea, and Taiwan. "Together," according to *Forbes*, "these tiny countries accounted for about $31 billion, or about one-quarter, of the US trade deficit last year."

French abortion pill *noun*
See RU 486.

fresh nugs *noun*
(*Teenage Slang*) A sexy, well-developed young woman.

friction costs *noun*
Expenses related to the purchase and sale of securities or other assets, including commissions, taxes, and bid/ask

spread and sometimes extending to contain restrictions on trading units and trading time. A Wall Street term.

fright mail *noun*
Direct mail marketing in which the mailing envelopes or packaging are designed to appear as if they contain important official government documents, in order to mislead the recipient and encourage opening. Common practices include stamping on the enveloped "Social Security Protection Bureau," so as to lure especially the elderly into reading the advertising literature it contains.

FSBO
Abbreviation used by real estate agents for "for sale by owner." See FIZZBO.

fullerine *noun*
See BUCKYBALL.

fundies *noun plural*
(*Slang*) Religious fundamentalists.

fuzz box *noun*
An electronic box that when hooked to a guitar allows a wide variety of musical sounds.

G

....

gafiate *verb*
(*Slang*) To take a vacation; rusticate. [From *get away from it all* + (*a*)*te*]

gag rule *noun*
A controversial federal regulation that prohibits physicians who are practicing in Title X federally funded family planning clinics from providing any information about abortion or even telling pregnant women that abortion is a legal option.

gaijin (gye-JEEN) *noun*
A Japanese term meaning "foreigner."

galette (guh-LETT) *noun*
A thin-crusted French pizza with a topping typically of bacon and onions or of slices of fruit, such as apples or pears.

garage pop *noun*
A form of popular music that combines elements of folk and rock and is characterized by an informal, unpretentious style. This music originated in the garages of private homes, where the bands playing it practiced for months before playing at local clubs.

garbage time *noun*
(*Slang*) The time left in a game where the score spread is so large and the outcome is so clear that both teams put in lesser players till the clock has run out.

gardenburger *noun*
A meatless hamburger made from vegetables, cheeses, egg whites, and various grains and nuts.

Gaspra *noun*
An asteroid, about 12 miles long and 8 miles wide, orbiting between the orbits of Mars and Jupiter. See KILLER ASTEROID.

gateway *noun*
See TELEPHONE GATEWAY.

Gaucher's disease (GO-shayz) *noun*
A genetically transmitted disease that primarily affects Jews of European extraction. Symptoms include the swelling of the liver and spleen, anemia, fatigue, and bone deficiencies. While Gaucher's disease has always been considered untreatable and is sometimes fatal, a recent breakthrough with the drug **Ceredase** is showing considerable promise in halting its progression or reducing some of the symptoms.

gazundering *noun*
A practice by which a buyer of a property, after signing the purchase contract but before the closing, bargains down the price. It is especially common in a weak housing market, where the seller may be swayed by the limited options available. *Gazundering* is a reversal of the British **gazumping,** the practice by which a seller raises the price on a property after a price has been agreed upon with a buyer.

geekoid *noun*
(*Slang*) A socially insignificant or unattractive person; nerd; dweeb; geek.

gender illusionist *noun*
A transvestite; cross-dresser. A bias-free term.

Generation X *noun*
A marketing and television programming category that includes people born after 1965. This generation has proven somewhat elusive in terms of identified interests, buying patterns, and television viewing habits.

generously cut *adjective*
Being overweight; fat. A bias-free, nonsizist word. See
NONSIZIST.

get a body *verb*
(*Slang*) To kill someone. An urban street gang term.

get a life *interjection*
Used to urge someone to become involved with the rest
of the world instead of being primarily self-absorbed or out
of touch.

getting run *noun*
(*Slang*) Having sex. An urban street term.

giant African snail *noun*
The world's largest snail, about the size of a baseball and
possessing 80,000 teeth that allow it to devour an entire
head of lettuce without stopping. They have recently become popular as pets but pose an enormous ecological problem if they are set free, since they are capable of causing
severe agricultural damage. Also called **African Snail.**

ginzy trading *noun*
A shady practice in which some commodities exchange
members can profit by giving customers two different prices
for the same buy and sell order.

give me a break *interjection*
Used to request that one's credulity not be strained, as in
the expression, "Give me a break. If I'm the one in charge,
then why are you trying to make all the decisions?" Often
spelled *gimme a break.*

glam *noun*

A variety of heavy metal music that is loud but showy and somewhat stylish. [Probably shortening of *glamour*] See METAL FUNK; SPEED METAL; THRASH.

glass ceiling *noun*

An unspoken but real limitation imposed especially on women and minorities who seek to improve their status in an organization.

Glyph *noun*

A new technology, developed by the Xerox Corporation, that adds a degree of "intelligence" to paper. The Glyph process creates a bar code that tells a computer where to look for special information that has been encoded on the paper. Glyph stores information as diagonal marks, allowing regular paper to serve as a data-storage medium that can be generated and read by computers. "The marks form a stipple pattern and can be used to carry data at different densities. . . . Glyph marks are generated by the computer using special software to transform typed information into special format." (*New York Times*)

GM-CSF *noun*

A hormone in the blood that is now believed to be responsible for dramatically decreasing cholesterol levels. [Abbreviation of Granulocyte-Macrophage Colony-Stimulating Factor]

gobbing *noun*

A practice originating at punk rock performances of spitting at a performer, often as a sign of appreciation. (Alex Smith, *New York Perspectives*)

GOCO *noun*

A system used especially by the federal government for the production of experimental planes and automobiles, new technologies, and military equipment. State and county governments are increasingly looking toward GOCO as a solution for retaining industry and jobs in their areas. [Acronym for **G**overnment-**O**wned, **C**ontractor-**O**perated (system)]

God Squad *noun*
Nickname for a US Cabinet-level committee that makes decisions regarding life-or-death policies on endangered species.

gold collar worker *noun*
Any of a corps of highly educated, high performing, decision-making workers who should constitute the work force of the future. [Coined by Professor Robert Kelly of Carnegie-Mellon University]

golden coffin *noun*
A benefits package payable to an executive's heirs upon his or her death. [Modeled on *golden parachute*]

golden handcuffs *noun plural*
Restraining pressures placed on middle-age executives who are unwillingly stuck in their positions for fear that making a move would cause a significant salary loss or decrease in fringe benefits. [By analogy with *golden handshake*]

goob *noun*
(*Slang*) A nerd; a jerk.

goodfella *noun*
(*Slang*) A gangster, especially a member of the Mafia. [Made popular by Martin Scorcese's 1991 film *Goodfellas*] Also called **wiseguy.**

good hejab (hee-JAB) *noun*
Proper Islamic dress. This includes standards of modesty, as exemplified by female head covering and loose-fitting clothing and completely nonflamboyant styling. Contrasted with **bad hejab.**

go-to guy *noun*
A reliable player a sports team can call on for the special effort needed to win, particularly during crunch time. See CRUNCH TIME.

GPS *noun*
A computerized technology for determining the position of an object anywhere in the world. Using a small hand-held receiver that picks up signals from a US satellite network, a person can instantly pinpoint his or her longitude and latitude anywhere in the world with an error range of less than 15 meters. [Abbreviation of Global Positioning System]

granny dumping *noun*
The abandonment of elderly, often infirm or ill persons by their families in an attempt to force the government to pay for care that the families cannot afford. Also called **grandpa dumping.**

Granny flat *noun*
An apartment built onto an existing residential property to house the elderly parents or grandparents of the home's residents.

Gravel Gerty *noun*
An underground bunker designed for the disassembly and temporary storage of decommissioned nuclear weapons. Designed for safety, its roof is layered aboveground with

tons of gravel to cushion any accidental detonations. [After *Gravel Gerty*, tough character in the comic strip "Dick Tracy," by Chester Gould]

green *adjective*
Of, relating to, or concerning environmental issues.

greenback green *noun*
A member of a demographically youthful group that spends heavily on environmental issues and financially supports products perceived as environmentally sound. [Derived from a poll taken by the Roper Organization]

green lobby *noun*
Any of the lobbying groups with common environmental interests, including Greenpeace, the Sierra Club, and Citizens for a Better Environment.

greenlock *noun*
Traffic gridlock common at national forests and parks especially during the summer tourist season. Attendance at national parks has increased regularly over the past fifteen years to a current level of 60 million visitors for the fifty national parks.

greenmail *noun*
See WHITEMAIL.

Green Mail *noun*
A proposed environmental fundraising plan by Brazil and Argentina that would be based on "an environmental stamp . . . to be used compulsorily in all international correspondence." (*New York Times*)

green marketing *noun*
Marketing efforts by large corporations to persuade the public that their products, packaging, manufacturing meth-

ods, and intentions are environmentally sound. The term refers to more than simply marketing a product; it is used just as much for marketing a corporate image. McDonald's, Proctor and Gamble, and Xerox, among others, have made strong efforts to position themselves as active environmentally concerned corporations, linking their products and services with environmental goals.

green product *noun*
A product that is or is said to be environmentally sound.

green revolution *noun*
The burgeoning environmental awareness and activity affecting the nation and having a profound impact in corporate planning and public relations efforts. See GREEN MARKETING; GREEN PRODUCT; GREENTAILING.

green seal *noun*
The so-called Good Earthkeeping seal of approval indicating that a product and its manufacture are not dangerous to the environment.

greentailing *noun*
A retail movement that focuses exclusively on environmental and ecological products. [From *green* + re*tailing*]

greenwashing *noun*
A corporation's disingenuous efforts to promote itself as an ecologically sensitive, pro-environmental force, often through advertising and promotional activities.

greenway movement *noun*
A conservation movement originating in the eastern United States whose goal is to retain for future park land and recreational purposes undeveloped patches and tracts

of land, large and small, in suburbs and in areas near cities as well as in more rural areas.

grindage *noun*
   (*Teenage Slang*) Food.

grouser *noun*
   Any of a group comprising about one-quarter of the US population whose concern about environmental issues is small. [Derived from a study done by the Roper Organization to determine how much more money environmentally aware consumers would be willing to pay for green products]

Grumpie *noun*
   Any of the 78 million Americans born after the Second World War and schooled during the cold-war years of the Eisenhower administration. [Abbreviation of Grown Up Mature Professionals]

grunt shows *noun*
   See TABLOID TV.

G-77 *noun*
   The 128 Third World countries' unified effort to deal with environmental matters. [The name is a play on **G-7,** the seven major nations including Canada, France, Germany, Great Britain, Italy, Japan, and the United States that handle most environmental matters] See AGENDA 21.

guerilla marketing *noun*
   A nontraditional marketing tactic that takes its marketing message to the streets where samples of the product might be handed out, immediate feedback recorded, con-

sumer questions answered, and good public relations established.

guided imagery *noun*
A relaxation technique in which a person is guided, either directly by a therapist or by using a specially prepared tape recording, to learn to reduce stress levels or to relieve chronic pain. Recently, this technique has been used to help patients visualize their immune and nervous systems as a means of sensing how the systems respond to particular stressors that cause a physical ailment or increase levels of pain associated with an ailment.

guideway *noun*
The electromagnetic equivalent of a train track, over which a magnet train levitates through magnetic force.

Gunderboom *noun*
An antipollution barrier system used on Long Island Sound that consists of a water-permeable perimeter curtain that hangs from a floating boom to the sea floor, keeping jellyfish and debris from entering swimming areas and beaches and filtering out algae.

GVHD *noun*
A potentially fatal complication following an organ transplant in which the foreign tissue produces its own rejection reaction to the host body, rather than the other way around. [Abbreviation of Graft-Versus-Host Disease]

g.w.r.b.i. *noun*
Baseball runs batted in that give a team a lead in a game that it doesn't lose. [Abbreviation of game-winning runs batted in]

Gyandzha (GAHN-juh) *noun*
The new Azerbaijani name for Kirovabad.

gym rat *noun*
A person whose intense efforts and long hours demonstrate an intense determination to win at all costs. A *Time* magazine article on Jay Leno described him as "the gym rat of comedians, the guy who practiced long after everyone else had gone home."

Hackey Sack *noun*
See FOOTBAG.

hairy potato *noun*
A hybrid edible potato that is a cross between the domestic potato and a wild inedible Bolivian species and has hairy foliage that traps plant pests, making the use of pesticides unnecessary.

haken *verb*
To go surfing and then have an afternoon meal. A term used by surfers, especially in California.

Halcion *noun*
A sleeping medication manufactured by the Upjohn Co. that has become the source of considerable controversy for its alleged side effects, including confusion, temporary memory loss, dizziness, and hyperexcitability.

hanger steak *noun*
A slightly sinewy but flavorful cut of steak from the flank area, near the kidneys.

happy camper *noun*
See UNHAPPY CAMPER.

hat act *noun*
(*Slang*) A good-looking, sexy country music performer, such as George Strait, who draws a predominantly college-age crowd.

hatchet *noun*
A controversial new oar design, three inches shorter and 20% larger than the standard design used in college rowing, recently introduced by the Dreissigacker brothers, whose firm is the largest manufacturer of sweep oars for competition rowing in the United States. "The new shape is called the Big Blade by the manufacturer and 'the hatchet' in college rowing circles. . . . The shape more resembles a meat cleaver than a small ax, but the later name has caught on." (William N. Wallace, *New York Times*)

headbanger *noun*
(*Slang*) An ardent fan of heavy metal music.

heads *noun plural*
(*Disparaging*) The floor workers at an assembly plant.

Healthy Start *noun*
A Federal program, introduced in the 1990s by President Bush, that according to the *Washington Post* "is designed to test ways to improve medical care and other services for women living in places that have high infant death rates." The ultimate goal of the $171 million program is to reduce

infant mortality by increasing the number of women who get prenatal care.

hedonic damages *noun*
Damages awarded in a civil suit for the loss of ability to enjoy life's pleasures.

Heisei era (HAY-SAY) *noun*
The current Japanese era marked by the ascension of Emperor Akihito.

hejab (hee-JAB) *noun*
See BAD HEJAB; GOOD HEJAB.

heli-exploring *noun*
The exploration of normally inaccessible areas of the Canadian Rockies by means of jet-powered helicopters. "With heli-exploring, age is no barrier: in the past ten years we have successfully catered to persons from 8 to 85, and on a regular basis, 60% of our guests are over 50." (catalog from Tauck Tours)

Helios *noun*
A new dry-process film system developed by the Polaroid Corporation that is based on carbon rather than silver-halide technology and uses a dry laser process to develop the film. "Helios can quickly create a hard-copy record of images captured by highly sophisticated scanning equipment used for medical testing and diagnosis. Once captured, the images are sent to a laser inside a Polaroid machine that is about the size of a mid-sized office copier." (*New York Times*)

helium heels *noun*
A woman who sleeps with a succession of men, each one in a progressively higher position of authority than his

predecessor. A sexist slang term, quoted in *Variety*'s "Buzz" column.

Herb *noun*
(*Slang*) A person who is easily intimidated or scared away; a wimp. An urban street term.

heterosexism *noun*
Oppression of those who have other than a heterosexual orientation.

hey *interjection*
Used to set off a thought, conclusion, observation, or insight in or as if in conversation, as in The New York State Lottery's recent slogan, "Hey, you never know."

high concept *adjective*
A Hollywood film whose main idea can be easily summarized in one sentence. For instance, films such as *Home Alone* and *Coming to America* are high concept films, driven by a simple plot line with character, motivation, and cinematic techniques as secondary considerations.

high performance file system *noun*
See HPFS.

hill rat *noun*
(*Slang*) A Congressional staffer.

HMR *noun*
See OPTIFAST.

home in *verb*
To stay securely at home. Often used to describe a situation where large numbers of people stay home, as from fear

of severe weather, a threat to health, or impending civil disorder, when they would otherwise be out.

homevid *noun*
Television, videocassette recorders, and video laser disk players used at home for entertainment. Also called **HV.**

honk *verb*
(*Teenage Slang*) To vomit.

horizontal drilling *noun*
A new method of oil and gas drilling in which a technologically advanced drill mechanism (the **horizontal drill**), under an engineer's command, curves as it descends through strata of rock until it is able to move horizontally through a layer of previously inaccessible rock. "The process," according to science writer Thomas C. Hayes, "is effective in geological formations where oil has been trapped in vertical fractures lying in the same layer. Because a drill from one well can reach so much more oil, the cost of recovering it drops considerably."

hose *verb*
(*Slang*) To spray with bullets from an automatic or semiautomatic weapon, as in, "We hosed them as they stood around on the corner." An urban street term.

house *verb*
(*Slang*) To steal money from, as in, "I housed him already. Leave him alone." An urban street term.

housed *adjective*
(*Teenage Slang*) Forced to stay at home, usually as a punishment; grounded.

H.O.V. *noun*
A vehicle carrying two or more passengers. In over a dozen states, H.O.V.s are given special express lanes, especially during rush hours, to encourage car-pooling and limit the number of single-passenger vehicles on the road. [Abbreviation of High Occupancy Vehicle]

HPFS *noun*
A computer disk management system developed by IBM that is presumably much more efficient than the traditional FAT (file allocation table) system used on most personal computers today. HPFS permits long file names (254 characters as opposed to the FAT's 8 characters) and assures much better management of disk space. [Abbreviation of High Performance File System] Also called **high performance file system.** See IFS.

huitlacoche (weet-la-КОН-chay) *noun*
An edible black fungus that is found on rotting corn and has become esteemed when used in such foods as pâté, soup, and crepes as served in fashionable restaurants.

human ecology *noun*
Home economics, as designated in some college and university course work.

humint (HYOO-mint) *noun*
Human intelligence, with reference to information provided by people rather than gained through computerized, electronic, or technical intelligence-gathering means. "A four-star general, describing the Army's intelligence efforts to locate and release our hostages, said, 'We had some assets that the CIA needed for humint,' referring to human intelligence. 'So we made them available for the (hostage) res-

cue operation.' " (George C. Wilson, *The Washington Post*) [From *hum*an + *int*elligence]

Hummer *noun*
A military vehicle noted for its ability to navigate through extremely rough terrain. The Hummer first gained general popularity during the Persian Gulf War. Recently, a modified civilian version that meets federal safety regulations has been offered to the public by a defense contractor, LTV. [From High-Mobility Multipurpose Wheeled Vehicle] Also called **Humvee.**

hurl *verb*
(*Slang*) To vomit.

HV *noun*
See HOMEVID.

hydrospeeding *noun*
A new water sport, similar to white-water rafting, in which the participant uses a cone-shaped piece of plastic, called a **boogie board,** in addition to fins, a padded wet suit, and helmet. It has become popular in France.

hype
(*Slang*) **1.** *noun* Dope. An urban street term frequently used in rap lyrics, as in, "Give me the hype and I'll be the type." **2.** *adjective* Really neat; cool. Used in songs and in advertising lyrics by rap singers such as Young MC.

hyperimmune *adjective*
Of or relating to newly patented farm animal products, such as milk and eggs, manipulated to contain human antibodies in addition to their usual nutrients. Stolle Research and Development, the inventors, say the products can be

tailored to fight tooth decay, strep throat, and other human ailments.

ice *noun*
An illegal drug that is a smokable version of methamphetamine. Also called **crystal meth.**

Iceberg system *noun*
A new computer storage system, from Storage Technology Corporation, that links together many smaller drives to replace the large drives traditionally used on mainframe computers, with the claimed advantages of increased speed and lower cost.

Iceland disease *noun*
See CHRONIC FATIGUE SYNDROME.

ice people *noun plural*
The descendants of northern Ice Age people, as designated by Dr. Leonard Jeffries, former head of the Afro-American Studies Department at the City University of New York. According to his controversial theory, the Ice people were materialistic, egotistical, and exploitive, as contrasted with the caring and humanistic **sun people** of Asia, Africa, Latin America, and the Caribbean.

idea software *noun*
A category of computer software with a variety of brainstorming tools and thinking aids, including outlining and

idea development programs, word association databases (rhyming words, synonyms, and the like), and free-text multifile searching, that allow the user to see connections between words, ideas, topics, subsections, or major subject headings.

IFS *noun*
A new computer architecture that will allow increased efficiency in the storing of information on a computer's hard disk. [Abbreviation of Installable File System] Also called **installable file system**. See HPFS.

inanfu *noun*
See COMFORT WOMEN.

incarcerated staff *noun*
Prison inmates who are assigned or leased to a company as independent contractors, usually as part of their rehabilitation process.

incontinent ordnance *noun*
Bombs and artillery shells that fall inconveniently short or wide of their targets and hit civilians, soldiers, or allies.

industrial disco *noun*
Dance music that combines synthesizer effects and pulsating rhythms and is often associated with a political philosophy that fuses punk and activism or terrorism. Also called **dancecore; Euro-body music.**

inflatable shoe *noun*
See PUMP INFLATABLE SHOE.

InfoClips *noun*
A new telephone service that provides cellular users with voice mail and local traffic, weather, and sports reports.

informated factory *noun*

A factory in which workers are given more authority and information about day-to-day operations than is the practice in traditional manufacturing facilities. Workers in these factories benefit from the advancements of automation and the Japanese philosophy of worker participation and "spend a significant part of their day collecting and sorting data about subjects like quality control, inventory and shipments, etc." (*New York Times*)

information gateway *noun*

See TELEPHONE GATEWAY.

initial public offering *noun*

The process of taking a privately held company public through the issuance of stock to the public.

ink tag *noun*

An antishoplifting device consisting of a plastic disk with chambers of indelible ink that spurts out if the tag is tampered with. The ink tag is attached to an item and can only be removed by a special tool.

in-line roller skate *noun*

A hybrid roller skate having a single line of rollers capable of providing speeds of up to 30 miles per hour.

installable file system *noun*

See IFS.

intelligent document *noun*

A paper document that contains compressed or coded information, readable by computers, in addition to standard text and graphics accessible to human readers. See GLYPH.

interactive book *noun*
See PAPERLESS BOOK.

Interactive Video and Data Services *noun*
See TWO-WAY TELEVISION.

interactive voice response *noun*
See IVR SYSTEM.

interactivity *noun*
A form of broadcast programming that allows viewers to participate by calling in while a show or event is in progress. A 900 number may be used for viewers to register their opinions on some issue, or callers may be asked to participate in a game show or dating show by calling in while the show is broadcasting.

internetworking *noun*
The process of connecting several branch offices of an organization to each other or to a home office through a local area network (LAN) of microcomputers linked by ordinary phone lines or high-speed optical data lines.

in the loop *adverb*
In a close relationship with associates who share information, consult, and act as a team.

in-your-face *adjective*
Rudely or aggressively confrontational. "Critics expect more consumer backlash against what they disdainfully call 'in-your-face media.'" (*Wall Street Journal*)

I.P.O.
Abbreviation of initial public offering.

Iridium system *noun*
The proprietary name for the world's largest and most complex satellite system, scheduled for completion in 1997.

It will consist of 77 orbital satellites and 20 or more ground stations connected by advanced digital cellular telephone technology to produce a worldwide cellular phone network.

ISDN *noun*
Telecommunications networks that allow high-speed sending and receiving of voice, video, fax, or other digital information either over regular telephone lines or from one computer to another. [Abbreviation of **I**ntegrated **S**ervices **D**igital **N**etworks]

ISEW (EYE-SO) *noun*
An alternative method of evaluating the overall health of an economy and the well-being of its inhabitants. The ISEW, according to H. Steven Dashefsky, "takes into account the cost of the depletion of renewable resources, the loss of farmland and wetlands, and the cost of water and air pollution. It also includes long-term factors, such as the impact of a product that damages the ozone layer or affects global warming." [Acronym for **I**ndex of **S**ustainable **E**conomic **W**elfare]

Issyk-Kul (ICE-ik-kul) *noun*
The new name for Rybachye, a city in Kyrgyzstan (formerly Kirghiz).

IVDS *noun*
See TWO-WAY TELEVISION.

IVR system *noun*
A new computerized telecommunications technology that allows a caller to route a call, make a request for information, order a product, or have a fax sent by pressing numbers on a keypad or through various voice-recognition

capabilities. [Abbreviation of Interactive Voice Response System] Also called **interactive voice response.**

Izhevsk (ee-SHEFSK) *noun*
The Russian city formerly known as Ustinov.

·····················

jakfruit *noun*
A South Asian fruit, the largest in the world to grow on a tree, that has recently become prized by gourmet cooks in the US.

jam *noun*
(*Slang*) The noise level of a party or event, as in, "Let's pump up the jam here." An urban street term.

jammer *noun*
See CULTURAL JAMMER.

Japan, Inc. *noun*
Japan viewed sometimes grudgingly as a highly successful post–World War II economic power.

Jell-O shot *noun*
A mixture of flavored gelatin and vodka served in a shot-sized paper cup or in the form of chilled cubes.

Jerusalem syndrome *noun*
A psychiatric condition affecting some tourists visiting Israel in which the sufferer becomes overwhelmed by the

spiritual power of the experience and begins to identify with a biblical character, such as King Solomon or Moses. See STENDAHL SYNDROME.

jet *verb*
(*Slang*) To leave; split. An urban street term.

jewel box *noun*
See ECO-PAK.

job lock *noun*
A situation in which a person stays in an otherwise undesirable job for the sole purpose of having health insurance coverage.

juice *noun*
(*Slang*) Power. An urban street term, notable in the 1992 film *Juice*. In reviewing the film in the *Detroit Free Press*, critic Robin D. Givhan explains what juice means to the inner-city youth who are the subjects of the film: "The line separating fear and anger disappears. The two become one. And their power becomes a single force, blinding to those who possess it and devastating to those unable to control it."

juice box *noun*
See DRINK BOX.

juku *noun*
A school that supplements regular schooling by teaching children how to pass rigorous and highly competitive entrance exams for higher education like those that determine future success in Japan. The jukus are flourishing in regions of the US with a large Japanese population. Also called **cram school.**

JumboTron *noun*
 A huge video screen, from 550 square feet to over 4000 square feet in area, that uses hundreds of TV picture tubes to generate a massive picture and is suited to public areas.

junior suite *noun*
 A large hotel room with a partition separating the bed and sitting areas.

junk phone *noun*
 The aggregate of 900-number phone lines offering a wide variety of services, among them friendship lines, confessional services, celebrity news and gossip, concert and theater reviews and listings, and sexually oriented talk.

junk science *noun*
 A miscellany of biased data, spurious inference, and logical nonsense sometimes presented in courtroom testimony by people whom the court accepts as expert witnesses, seen to cause a surge in baseless claims and frivolous suits that result in hugely costly settlements bankrupting some companies and contributing to skyrocketing malpractice premiums. [Coined by legal scholar Peter Huber, in his book *Galileo's Revenge*]

Kabanger *noun*
 See KLICKSTICK.

ka-ching *interjection*
 Used in mimicry of the sound of a cash register to suggest the opportunity of making large sums of money.

kaizen (kye-ZEHN) *noun*
A Japanese term meaning "constant improvement," now used internationally to indicate worker-instituted productivity and performance improvements, especially in manufacturing. The word and concept have come into use in the US as Japanese auto makers begin to build large plants here.

Kaleida *noun*
A joint venture by IBM and Apple Computer to develop a standardized multimedia computer that will feature compact disk graphics and digital sound.

kangaroo care *noun*
Infant care that encourages a level of bonding between parent and child that is often precluded in the neonatal intensive care nursery. Inspired by the behavior of marsupials, who nurture their young in their pouches, kangaroo care is said to facilitate at-risk infants' psychological development and self-esteem by allowing them to be carried, fed, and touched by their mothers or surrogates in a sterile and safe environment.

karoshi (kah-ROE-shee) *noun*
A Japanese term meaning "death from overwork." In a 1992 Reuters story, the Japanese Defense Council for Victims of Karoshi said that as many as 10,000 Japanese work themselves to death every year.

Keck I *noun*
A giant telescope, with a 10-meter mirror constructed of 36 separate segments, located near the pollution-free peak of Mauna Kea, on Hawaii. Its twin, the **Keck II,** is scheduled to be in operation by 1996. "Collectively, this new generation of ground-based instruments will open an extraordinary new window on the cosmos. What we can look forward

to," says Caltech astronomer Maarten Schmidt, "is the biggest gain in telescope power in the past 50, maybe even 100 years."

keiretsu (kay-REH-tsoo) *noun*
The Japanese name for the giant interlinked companies that have driven Japan's postwar business successes. "The Americans tried to break up zaibatsu, the business groups that fueled prewar expansion. But . . . they were reconstituted in slightly altered form as keiretsu." (*Business Week*)

kenbei (KEN-bay) *noun*
A Japanese term, coined by novelist Yasua Tanaka, denoting a general contempt for America.

Kharagouli (kar-uh-GOO-lee) *noun*
The Georgian city formerly known as Ordzhonikidze.

Khodzhent (koh-JENT) *noun*
The city formerly known as Leninabad, in Tajikistan on the left bank of the Syr Darya River.

kiddie porn *noun*
Sexually explicit photos, films, or videos of children.

kidvid *noun*
Television programming for children, identified as a specific market segment. Also called **kideo.**

killer asteroid *noun*
Any of various large asteroids that, were they to strike the earth, would cause massive damage. "In 1989," according to columnist Dan Rattiner, "an asteroid almost a mile across came hurtling through the solar system and crossed the earth's path just a few million miles away." It is believed by

many geologists, based on their findings of shattered quartz crystals embedded in ancient shale deposits, that such an asteroid did hit the earth about 65 million years ago, possibly bringing about the extinction both of the dinosaurs and much of the plant life on the planet. See SHOCKED QUARTZ.

killer card *noun*
Any of a genre of trading cards featuring mass murderers and serial killers and including graphic depictions of their crimes. Many states have acted to ban the sale of these cards to minors.

kit food *noun*
See MEAL KIT.

Klickstick *noun*
A popular toy consisting of a plastic rod from which two small balls connected by plastic strings can be made to spin around and knock into each other, producing a clicking noise. According to *Time* magazine, over 4 million of them were sold in 1990. Also called **clacker; Kabanger.**

knowledge-based compensation *noun*
See SKILL-BASED PAY.

Kobe beef (KOH-bee, KOH-bay) *noun*
Beef produced from Wagyu bulls. [After *Kobe*, city in Japan] See WAGYU BULL.

Kumayri (koo-MY-ree) *noun*
The northwest Armenian city formerly known as Leninakan.

Kyrgyzstan (kur-ghee-STAN) *noun*
The new name for the former Soviet republic of Kirghiz, a mountainous region adjacent to China.

L

L

Abbreviation for liquidity. "While most people have learned to watch growth in the M1 money supply (checking accounts, currency, etc.), M2 or M3 indicators, some experts these days are staring at a figure that the Federal Reserve Board simply calls L, for liquidity." (John Crudele, *New York Post*)

lanai (luh-NYE) *noun*

A hotel room with a balcony or patio overlooking a body of water, as a bay or the ocean, and a decorative courtyard or a garden.

lap dancing *noun*

A form of table dancing in which a nude dancer dances within a few inches of a customer and concludes by sitting on the customer's lap in exchange for a tip. See TABLE DANCING.

Latvia *noun*

A former republic of the Soviet Union that is now an independent country recognized by the UN.

LEAP *noun*

A newly created market in long duration options, which can last as long as two years, as opposed to the traditional short-term options, which last for up to nine months. [Acronym for long-term equity anticipations]

learning circle *noun*

A concept in distance education in which classes around the world are connected on-line to collaborate on a specific curriculum or to work jointly on a project. See AG*SAT; DISTANCE EDUCATION.

Left Coast *noun*

The West Coast of the US.

lifetime telephone number *noun*

See EASY REACH 700.

light chip *noun*

A new generation of integrated circuits on a single chip in which information, instead of traveling through silicon pathways of electron energy, is transmitted far more efficiently through ceramic pathways of light energy. Also called **OEIC.**

lights-out factory *noun*

A theoretical factory of the future that will be so efficiently automated that it will be able to operate in the dark, unattended by human personnel.

Linda *noun*

A computer language developed by Lawrence Livermore Laboratory scientist David Gelertner and designed to link a number of computers to work together on a single task or problem. [Named after Linda Lovelace, former actress in the blue movie *Deep Throat,* a bit of irony on Gelertner's part, since a previous computer language was named ADA, after Ada Lovelace, the first woman programmer] See MASSIVELY PARALLEL PROCESSING.

liquid coal *noun*

An emulsion of bitumen and water, marketed under the name Orimulsion, that serves as an inexpensive fuel. Its advantages are achieved by combining the convenience of liquid oil with the cost effectiveness of hard coal.

Liski (LEE-skee, LYEE-skee) *noun*
The Russian city formerly known as Georgiu-Dezh.

Lithuania *noun*
A former republic of the Soviet Union that is now an independent country.

living needs benefits *noun*
A new option in life insurance that allows ill and dying policyholders to draw cash benefits while still living in order to pay for surgery or other medical expenses, according to Catherine Liden of the Gannett News Service. This option was originated by Prudential Insurance Co. of America's CEO, Ron D. Barbaro, at their Canadian division in 1990, and is now available through 60 US insurance companies. Also called **accelerated death benefits; living life insurance.**

loin of fish *noun*
The prime or center cut of a large fish, such as tuna, halibut, or swordfish, as newly described on some restaurant menus.

lo-life *noun*
(*Slang*) A youth who has a reputation for stealing Ralph Lauren Polo products from stores. [From Po*lo* + *life*, a play on *lowlife*, an immoral person]

longbox *noun*
A cardboard box, 6″ by 12″, used to package a compact disk for display and sale. Longboxes are gradually being abandoned because they waste natural resources.

long-term care *noun*
A comprehensive range of health, social, and support services designed to meet the needs of people who have a chronic disability. See CATASTROPHIC CARE.

lookism *noun*
An inclination to judge people by their perceived attractiveness, dress, or other physical characteristics.

Los Angelization *noun*
The rapid, unplanned, and poorly controlled growth of an area's population, with attendant traffic congestion, violent crime, overtaxing of resources and services, environmental pollution and land damage, and other social and economic problems. See PLAN.

LULUs
Acronym for **L**ocally **U**ndesirable **L**and **U**ses.

Lviv (luh-VEEF) *noun*
The Ukrainian city formerly known as Lvov.

M

Macaca nemestrina (ma-KAK-a) *noun*
A light brown southeast Asian monkey that is the only known nonhuman species other than the chimpanzee capable of being infected with the AIDS virus. It is currently being used in the development of an AIDS–HIV vaccine. Also called **pigtail macaque.**

Macedonia *noun*
A former republic of Yugoslavia that declared its independence in September 1991.

machoflops *noun*
(*Slang*) The ability of a computer chip to perform several trillion calculations per second. A computer hacker's term. See TERAFLOP.

mad cow disease *noun*
A fatal brain disease of cattle, bovine spongiform encephalopathy, that has recently caused beef shortages in various parts of the world.

magalog *noun*
A cross between a catalog and magazine with articles, features, and editorials focused on the products being sold. Lands' End, a major clothing catalog house, was one of the first to publish a magalog, adding employee profiles and travel tips to its basic catalog to make it appear more like a magazine. Also called **catazine.**

magnet train *noun*
A Japanese train that runs on a bed of air above the tracks, magnetically levitated by repelling superconductive magnets.

maintenance hatch *noun*
A manhole. A gender-neutral term.

mall brat *noun*
(*Slang*) Any of the middle to upper-middle class youths between the ages of 11 and 17 whose tastes include the music of Michael Jackson and the clothing of mall stores

like Chess King, and who are regarded by advertisers and merchandisers as comprising a new target market.

mall rat *noun*
(*Slang*) Any adolescent who uses a shopping mall as a hangout after school and on weekends.

mall walking *noun*
Exercise in the form of fast walking through the empty corridors of a shopping mall, usually early in the morning before the mall is open for business.

mamey (muh-MAY) *noun*
A tropical fruit that is roughly the size of a mango and has sandpapery brown skin and sweet, somewhat pungent flesh. Also called **sapote**.

M & A *noun*
A department in a law firm, investment house, or other institution that is devoted to corporate mergers, acquisitions, and takeovers. [Abbreviation of Mergers & Acquisitions]

Manglish *noun*
Feminist Varda One's term for "the English language as it is used by men in the perpetuation of male supremacy."

Mariupol (mar-ee-oo-pawl) *noun*
The Ukrainian city formerly known as Zhdanov.

Martvili (mar-TFIL-ee) *noun*
The Georgian city formerly known as Gegechkori.

Mashkan-shapir *noun*
A fabled lost city of Mesopotamia, the remains of which were recently discovered by Dr. Elizabeth Stone, an archae-

ologist from the State University of New York at Stony Brook. The original city flourished 4000 years ago and is situated in Southern Iraq between the Tigris and Euphrates rivers.

massively parallel processing *noun*
A technique in data processing in which a supercomputer, configured with anywhere from 32 to 16,000 microprocessors operating simultaneously, works on a single task to arrive at a solution in record time. Also called **parallel processing**. See CONNECTION MACHINE; LINDA.

maxi-sled *noun*
An aerodynamically advanced, ocean-racing boat measuring between 66 and 68 feet, "the new breed of speedy, responsive monohull yacht that is taking the California sailing crowd by storm and inspiring America's Cup designs." (Susan Price, *M* magazine) Also called **ULDB.**

MBO *noun*
The process whereby a company is purchased by its management, typically with borrowed money that uses the company's assets as collateral, allowing for the future possibility of discharging the debt and realizing a profit by liquidating the company. [Abbreviation of Management Buy-Out]

McPaper *noun*
(*Slang*) A college term paper written at the last minute and without much research or thought. [By analogy with *McDonald's,* a chain of fast-food restaurants]

MCS *noun*
A theory that exposure to certain chemicals, either individually or combined, can pose previously undetected

health risks for many people. [Abbreviation of Multiple Chemical Sensitivities]

MD *noun*
See MINIDISC.

M-Diesel *noun*
A new fuel made from methanol and cooking oil that is inexpensive to produce and is being considered as a substitute for diesel fuel.

MD player *noun*
See MINIDISC.

MD-12 *noun*
A jumbo four-engine passenger jet developed by the McDonnell Douglas Corporation to compete with Boeing's redoubtable 747. It is to be introduced in 1997 and will be able to fly 8000 miles without refueling and carry 430 passengers.

meal kit *noun*
A heat-and-serve meal with ingredients fully prepared before packaging and including such fare as pizza and tuna salad. Also called KIT FOOD.

means testing *noun*
A controversial proposal, as recently applied to Medicare and Social Security benefits, for basing a recipient's benefits on income rather than on the amount one has paid in over the years, the number of years worked, or on a fixed-rate rule.

MediFast *noun*
See OPTIFAST.

megachurch *noun*
Any of various religious congregations of several thousand members in which pastoral training, bible study, and

general educational, recreational, and social or philanthropic services supplement prayer meetings. Services of these churches are often televised by satellite or cable to distant parishioners.

memcon *noun*
A confidential memorandum, usually summarizing the results of a meeting. [From *mem*orandum and *con*fidential]

menu de dégustation (muh-NOO duh day-goos-ta-SYOHN) *noun*
A menu listing dinners consisting of six or seven coordinated courses. [French, tasting menu] Also called **tasting menu.**

metal funk *noun*
A critically esteemed variety of heavy metal music. See GLAM; SPEED METAL; THRASH.

Michelangelo virus *noun*
A computer virus that was first detected in Germany and quickly spread throughout the world's interlinked computer systems, within months being found on thousands of PCs in schools, offices, and homes in the United States. [So named because it was timed to begin destroying computer data on March 6, 1992, the birthday of Michelangelo]

mick *noun*
Minute. Used in the military, as in, "Give me five micks to bring this off." [By alteration and shortening of *minute*]

microbrewery *noun*
A small brewery, usually in a specialized restaurant or bar called a **brew pub** where the brewed product, such as beer, is sold. Also called **micro.**

microbubbles *noun*
Microscopic bubbles that are found under the ocean's surface and act as miniature loudspeakers in amplifying underwater sounds. See ACOUSTIC OCEANOGRAPHY.

microcar *noun*
A tiny city car, 4.5 feet by 8.2 feet, that is powered by battery and can carry two passengers at speeds of up to 30 mph. Something of a cross between a motor bike and an automobile, it is made and marketed in France. Also called **VSP.**

microcell *noun*
A smaller coverage area designed to augment the larger metropolitan cells in cellular telephone communication, making possible calls inside buildings and in less accessible parts of the calling area.

microfiber *noun*
A synthetic polyester-based fiber prized for its light weight, softness, and ability to fall with suppleness around the contours of the body.

microkernal *noun*
A self-contained part of a larger computer program, such as a computer's operating system, or of another larger system, such as the controller unit for a audio-video setup.

microloan *noun*
A government sponsored small-business loan made to third-world entrepreneurs who would usually not qualify for more traditional loan products.

micromachine *noun*
Any of various miniaturized mechanical devices, including gears, sensors, pumps, and other machine parts, that are

small enough to fit into a human capillary. These machines can be used to perform delicate surgical procedures in the areas where surgeons cannot reach or to make sensitive measurements and perform delicate maneuvers in space.

micro-marketing *noun*
A new form of traditional niche marketing in which small but clearly definable segments of a larger market, such as the pre-teen sneaker market or the over-65 car market, are identified. Also called **particle marketing.**

micromotor *noun*
A miniaturized motor, about the width of a human hair, used in micromachines. These motors require very little power and generate mechanical actions in extremely tiny areas. See MICROMACHINE.

microrobot *noun*
Any of various small robotic devices that use micromotors to accomplish a variety of infinitesimally small actions. Microrobots are used in delicate medical procedures.

MiniDisc *noun*
A 2½-inch compact disk developed by Sony on which can be recorded the same 74 minutes of sound as on a larger CD. Although it has slightly less accuracy and range than the CD, it is capable of recording as well as playing and can be carried around and played on an **MD player,** which is not much larger than a pack of cigarettes. Also called **MD.**

MIPS *noun*
(*Slang*) Mental alertness, as in, "I'm on low MIPS today because of my busy weekend." [From a computer acronym for **M**illions of **I**nstructions **P**er **S**econd]

modem sharing *noun*
 A new computer software technology that allows multiple users on a network to share a single modem.

moguls racing *noun*
 An olympic downhill speed skiing event in which the skier must navigate a quarter-mile course marked by moguls and other rough terrain. Also called **bump racing.**

Moldova (mawl-DOH-vuh) *noun*
 The eastern European republic formerly known as Moldavia.

momentum investing *noun*
 An investment strategy in which money is invested in stocks whose price is unnaturally accelerating because of a rapid but potentially short-lived double-digit increase in earnings.

momentum investor *noun*
 One who engages in momentum investing. "Momentum investors try to hitch a ride on stocks that are accelerating in price because the company's earnings are growing at a double-digit rate. But the flip side is that the slightest hint of stiffer competition, production snags, or slower sales can cause nearly instantaneous markdowns in the stocks." (*Wall Street Journal*)

monoclonal imaging *noun*
 A diagnostic technique in which laboratory-produced antibodies are introduced into a patient's body to determine the location of a tumor, dead heart tissue, or other disease site, thus providing an accurate picture of the pathology.

Monte Carlo simulation *noun*
 A statistical technique in sampling and polling in which random numbers are used to simulate unpredictable behav-

iors and decisions and are then compared to empirical results to determine the effects of different factors on the
decision-making process.

Montenegro (mahn-tuh-NEE-grow) *noun*
A former republic of Yugoslavia that formed the Federal
Republic of Yugoslavia with Serbia in April 1992.

moon rock *noun*
(*Slang*) An illegal drug that is a mixture of heroin and
crack. Also called **speedball; parachute.**

morcellator *noun*
A device used in videoscopic surgery that pulverizes an
organ, such as a kidney, while a vacuum attachment sucks
out the contents, avoiding the necessity of making a large
incision on the patient. See VIDEOSCOPIC SURGERY.

morning-after pill *noun*
See RU 486.

morphing *noun*
A computer animation technique in which an object is
made to change shape in front of the viewer's eyes, its contours and colors transforming fluidly. The technique is
widely used in advertising, as in one TV commercial in
which a speeding car evolves swiftly into a tiger by means
of morphing.

morphmania *noun*
Intense fascination in the advertising world with computer morphing.

Moses *noun*
A political candidate who is seen to be metaphorically
roaming the desert of the talk show circuit instead of focus-
ing on specific issues.

motivationally deficient *adjective*
Lazy. A bias-free term that seeks to focus responsibility on society rather than on the individual.

mousemilking *noun*
(*Slang*) The investing of maximum time and effort for minimum return, as on an academic project, business venture, or in trying to sell or service a client.

MPC *noun*
An integrated system consisting of a personal computer with a built-in CD drive. [Abbreviation of Multimedia Personal Computer] Also called **multimedia computer.**

M.R.E. *noun*
A food product that is packaged in a thick plastic pouch, can be consumed without heating or other preparation, and provides at least 1400 calories and the appropriate balance of nutrients and vitamins. Used especially in the military. [Abbreviation of Meals, Ready to Eat.]

MTBE *noun*
A non-ethanol petroleum-based gasoline additive that reduces carbon monoxide emissions. [Abbreviation of Methyl Tertiary Butyl Ether]

Mukhabarat (moo-ha-bah-RAT) *noun plural*
The secret police of Syria.

mule *noun*
A drug courier who typically conceals the drug stash in latex condoms packed in the intestines or other part of the body. The mules became widely known following the crash of a Colombian airline in New York City, when surgical

teams treating the survivors discovered 74 sealed drug-filled condoms in the intestinal tracts of two of the patients.

multiculturalism *noun*
   The evenhanded treatment or study of the history and culture of all ethnic and racial groups, as in education and textbook publishing.

multimedia computer *noun*
   See MPC.

multithread *adjective*
   Of, relating to, or being a software programming technique that allows a computer to process different tasks simultaneously by sharing the power of a microprocessor.

multivalve engine *noun*
   A technically advanced automobile engine designed by the Japanese that is more fuel-efficient and more powerful per pound than the engines used in American automobiles. By adding extra valves to each of the cylinders, the engine can ignite more fuel more quickly, thus producing faster and stronger cylinder strokes.

mush-core pornography *noun*
   Deliberately erotic content, as in advertisements for Calvin Klein jeans, the rock videos of Madonna, or *Sports Illustrated*'s swimsuit issue. [Coined by Ben Yagoda, *New York Observer*]

mushroom *noun*
   A victim of a stray bullet, especially in shootouts on city streets or in crowded areas.

N

narbo *noun*
(*Slang*) An uninteresting person; square.

NDE *noun*
An experience recalled by a person who came very close to death but then recovered. "The typical NDE has five stages: (1) you experience a sense of peace; (2) you have the sense of leaving your body and observing it from afar . . . (3) you enter a tunnel or 'darkness'; (4) you see a light at the end of the tunnel; and finally (5) you enter the light. Often at some point during the process you see your life pass before your eyes." (Cecil Adams) [Abbreviation of Near-Death Experience] Also called **near-death experience.**

nebby *noun, plural* **nebbies**
A member of a growing segment of financially troubled professional and managerial households headed by people between the ages of 35 and 54. According to national real-estate columnist Kenneth R. Harney, nebbies have "annual incomes above $55,000, nice houses, nice cars, and solid positions in their communities. They prospered in the 1980s and tapped their generous home equities to finance home additions, boats, vacation condos, and other luxuries. They cashed in part of their inflation winnings, in effect, just before the economic bust hit town. Now they're up to — or over — their earlobes in debt." [From **n**egative-**e**quity **b**aby **b**oomer + y]

neurotrophic factor *noun*
Any of a class of human proteins responsible for nerve growth, recently synthesized in laboratories with the hope of treating a variety of nerve diseases, such as Parkinson's disease and Alzheimer's disease. Some of the synthesized versions of this factor include Neurotrophin-3, CEP-427, and glial growth factor, each of which has shown some promise in slowing nerve damage in the elderly and neuropathically ill.

new age beverage *noun*
A natural fruit-flavored beverage with a carbonated water or an iced tea base. These beverages are perceived to be healthier than traditional carbonated sodas and artificial fruit punches, which contain chemical dyes and flavor enhancers.

New Conservation *noun*
The collective farming, ranching, and other business endeavors that are guided by an ecological viewpoint emphasizing the delicate and often precarious balance between the human inhabitants of a region and its flora and fauna. See BIORESERVE; ECO-RANCHING.

New Despotism *noun*
A concept developed by former President Richard Nixon during the 1992 presidential election to describe a burgeoning international repression that he believes will follow from the fall of international communism.

new hedonism *noun*
A sensuous approach in music in which instruments, including synthesizers, are used to explore new areas of sound. New hedonism is characteristic of the work of such modern composers as Morton Subotnick and Ezra Laderman.

New News *noun*
A new culture of journalistic information, what *Rolling Stone* calls "a heady concoction, part Hollywood film and TV, part pop music and pop art, mixed with popular culture and celebrity magazines, tabloid telecasts, cable, and home video." According to journalist and social commentator Bill Moyers, "The New News is seizing the function of mainstream journalism, sparking conversation and setting the country's social and political agenda."

New World Order *noun*
Collective security and other interests among formerly mutually hostile nations, as designated by the Bush administration.

NFP *noun*
A birth control philosophy and method sponsored and promoted by the Roman Catholic Church. NFP includes the **Billings mucus method.** [Abbreviation of Natural Family Planning]

nicotine patch *noun*
A transdermal patch that allows the slow steady absorption of nicotine through the skin. It is used to help smokers withdraw gradually from addiction to nicotine.

NIMBYism *noun*
An attitude of community resistance to the placing of toxic waste disposal sites or nuclear power plants within the community's borders. [Acronym for **N**ot **I**n **M**y **B**ack-**Y**ard + *ism*]

nine *noun*
(*Slang*) A nine-millimeter semi-automatic revolver, now becoming the weapon of choice for police departments countrywide. Used with *the*.

Nizhni Novogorod (NEEZH-nee NAWV-guh-rod) *noun*
The Russian city formerly known as Gorky.

Noah Principle *noun*
A principle in environmentalism and conservation that each species, no matter how important or unimportant to the ecological balance, has an equal right to exist, in view of which the government should not dedicate more money and effort to saving one species than another.

no-brainer *noun*
(*Slang*) A question or problem that requires little or no intelligent thought.

node *noun*
A computer that serves as a switchboard for online systems and the callers who are trying to reach them.

noise-rock *noun*
A rebellious form of rock music, popularized during the mid 1970s, that included the sounds of clanging cans, combustion engines, and grinding machinery.

non-ist *noun*
A person who rather self-righteously avoids foods, activities, and environments that might be even remotely harmful to the health.

nonsizist *adjective*
Of, relating to, or constituting language that seeks to be nonjudgmental in referring to a person's relative physical bulk. Words such as *thin, svelte, large,* and *fat* can be regarded as undesirable in nonsizist language. See GENEROUSLY CUT.

NORC *noun*
   A place in which half the residents are over 60 years of age, but which was not designed originally for an elderly population. [Abbreviation of Naturally Occurring Retirement Community]

not! *interjection*
   Derived from the usage of the popular TV and film characters of *Wayne's World*, this negation is added to the end of a statement to indicate emphatic contradiction, as in, "I really think you're beautiful. Not!"

notch reform bills *noun plural*
   Proposed federal legislation to correct an alleged inequity in Social Security benefits received by retirees born between 1917 and 1922.

nuch *noun*
   (*Slang*) Not much. A contraction popular among West Coast surfers.

nuclear football *noun*
   The set of electronic controls that are carried at all times by a traveling chief of state and serve as the ignition for a process by which nuclear response can be quickly initiated in times of an emergency. [From being likened to a thrown football that requires a receiver to take the next necessary action]

Nugget *noun*
   An Australian gold coin that weighs over two pounds and is said to be the largest coin the world.

Nunavut *noun*
   A 772,000-square-mile section of Canada's Northwest Territories that is set for independent political control by

the Inuit by 1999. "Nunavut" means "our land" in the Inuit language.

nutriceutical *noun*
Any food of the category that includes natural food products such as fish, oils, and oat bran. These products are believed to yield medical benefits in addition to nutrition. [From *nutri*tion + pharma*ceutical*] Also called **pharm food.**

object *noun*
See PINK.

object linking *noun*
See OLE.

October surprise *noun*
An alleged plot in which Republican presidential candidate Ronald Reagan and the leaders in Iran were suspected of agreeing to delay the release of American hostages being held in Iran until after the presidential election of 1980, thereby helping achieve a Republican victory, as suggested by Columbia University professor Gary Sick, a former staff member of the National Security Council under three presidents.

OEIC *noun*
See LIGHT CHIP. [Acronym for **o**pto**e**lectronic **i**ntegrated **c**ircuit]

okey-doke *noun*
(*Slang*) A fake move; feint. An urban street term.

OLE *noun*
A computer software technique in which one program can borrow some of the specialized capabilities of another; for example, a word processing program can borrow some of the powerful graphics capabilities of a presentation or drawing program. [Acronym for **O**bject **L**inking and **E**mbedding] Also called **object linking.**

olim (oh-LEEM) *noun plural*
Jewish people who immigrate to Israel under the law of return.

1-alphahydroxy-vitamin D2 *noun*
A patented variant of vitamin D produced from plants that is used to prevent bone loss without causing excessive buildup of calcium in the body.

180 out *adjective*
(*Military Slang*) Completely wrong, false, or fabricated, as in, "That answer is 180 out."

one-number service *noun*
A telephone number that identifies a person rather than a location and can be used to instruct the phone service of the person's location at a given time.

on-hold music *noun*
A telemarketing service by which a caller ordering tickets to a concert can also order the performer's latest recording.

on line *noun*
A stage in the fraternity pledging or hazing process.

on-scene show *noun*
A television program in which a camera crew is sent to a scene of a crime, accident, or other grisly event to record

the reactions of participants or bystanders or in which the event is reenacted as if it were happening live.

ooze ball *noun*
Volleyball played in mud, as at Tulane University in New Orleans, Louisiana.

opal
Acronym for **O**lder **P**erson with **A**ctive **L**ifestyle, **O**lder **P**ersons with **A**ctive **L**ifestyles.

open adoption *noun*
A form of adoption in which the biological parents and adoptive parents are either known to each other or become known to each other in the adoption process. See CLOSED ADOPTION.

open jaw *noun*
A roundtrip planned by a travel agency in which the return trip begins at a point other than the arrival point, as in the case of a passenger who flies from New York to San Francisco but flies back from Seattle to New York. [From the resemblance of the route to an open jaw]

optical molasses *noun*
A technology developed at AT&T Bell Laboratories that uses light to create an electromagnetic force that can bring atoms to a still state, allowing them to be observed, manipulated, or transformed into a new type of matter.

optical tweezers *noun*
A new laser-based technology that allows scientists to seize, hold, or manipulate sub-microscopic and organic structures. "Among other things, optical tweezers can keep a tiny organism swimming in place while scientists study its paddling flagella under a microscope." (*Time*)

Optifast *noun*

A weight-loss food product, manufactured by the Sandoz Nutrition Corporation, consisting of a low-calorie, high-protein powdered formula or liquid beverage. Sales of liquid protein have grown to $5 billion a year since 1970, according to writer Jennifer Stoffel. Similar products marketed under different brand names include **BaylorFast, Medifast,** and **HMR.**

opt-in provision *noun*

A provision in credit card and privacy laws that would specifically require a cardholder to authorize the use of information in his or her files before it is shared with other interested parties.

organoid *noun*

An organlike structure that appears capable of mimicking specific functions within the body. "The first organoid . . . consisted of liver cells that were able to maintain themselves and develop a vascular system after implantation in rats." (*Insight*)

oriented strand board *noun*

An engineered wood product manufactured by gluing together wood flakes from small trees that formerly were unusable for lumber products.

Orimulsion *noun*

A trade name for liquid coal. See LIQUID COAL.

orphan drug *noun*

A pharmaceutical product that is used to treat diseases that affect relatively few patients and is therefore less profitable to market. Drugs such as Erythropoietin for severe anemia and Human Growth Hormone for dwarfism are two such products. To promote research into these orphan drugs, the federal government has provided various financial subsidies and incentives to encourage research and experimentation.

Oso sweet *noun*
A new variety of large sweet onion imported from South America.

OS/2 *noun*
The IBM microcomputer operating system designed to replaced the original DOS. OS/2 is graphically based, compatible with Windows, and allows the transfer of data between different programs. [Acronym for **O**perating **S**ystem-**2**]

out *verb*
To expose secrets about (someone) publicly. [From the practice by a few gays of publicly revealing the sexuality of prominent gay people who prefer to retain their privacy]

outlet mall *noun*
A mall made up primarily of manufacturers' retail outlet stores, at which the manufacturers' own brands of merchandise are discounted.

out-of-pocket payment *noun*
Money paid by a patient for health care not covered by either public or private insurance. The term refers to both deductible and coinsurance payments, as well as to payments for noncovered products and services.

outsert *noun*
A supplement to a magazine or newspaper, usually wrapped in a separate polybag and distributed with the periodical.

outsider art *noun*
Art works produced by amateur or professional artists who are outside the mainstream. Outsider art "can include traditional quilts and the productions of self-taught Sunday painters, the work of the retarded, the insane, the 'primitive,' the uneducated — anyone not part of the big-city art world." (*Wall Street Journal*) Also called **raw art; visionary art.**

outtake show *noun*
A television show constructed mainly from small sound and video bites of real life that are spliced together with a central theme and narrative. One example, "America's Funniest Home Videos," quickly became one of TV's top ten network shows.

over the top *adjective*
Being extreme in character; outrageous, as in, "A stand-up comic whose style is over the top."

Ozurgeti *noun*
The Georgian city formerly known as Makharadze.

. . . .

Pac-Man counterattack *noun*
See PEOPLE PILL.

Pai-gow (PIE-gow) *noun*
A Chinese gambling game, involving dice and small plastic tiles, currently popular on the West Coast and in other sections of the country with a large Asian population.

paintball wars *noun*

A game that gained popularity during the recent economic downturn, possibly as a form of discharging aggression and frustration. The game is played outdoors, in woods or fields, usually in teams of 10 to 30 adult players. The goal is for each team to guard its own flag while trying to capture the opponent's flag and to take it to their home position. Participants wear goggles and face masks and use guns that fire paint-filled gelatin shells.

palmtop computer *noun*

A portable microcomputer that weighs under three pounds and is smaller in dimensions than a standard letter size sheet of paper. Palmtop computers serve primarily as electronic organizers, with an electronic address book, a calculator, an appointment calendar, and a clock.

pan music *noun*

Steel band music popular on the Caribbean islands of Trinidad and Tobago. The instruments used for this music consist of sections cut from old oil drums with resonant domes carefully hammered into the surface to produce a remarkable range of pitches and sonorities.

pantethine (PAN-tuh-thin) *noun*

A protein that is found in human cells and has been identified as instrumental in preventing other proteins in the lens of the eyes from clumping together and forming cataracts.

paperless book *noun*

A book published on a computer-readable medium, such as a disk, and read on a computer screen that has been especially designed to emulate in its black and white color and its size the printed page of a regular book. Among the advantages are quick forward or backward scanning and word and context searching. Also called **computer book; electronic book; interactive book.**

paperless design *noun*
   The process of designing an object, as an airplane or automobile, entirely on computer screens, without the use of drawings, schematics, or engineering diagrams on paper. The Boeing 777 jet, to be released in 1995, is the first fully engineered and designed airliner produced by paperless design.

paperless office *noun*
   A much-publicized concept that experts now realize will probably never come to fruition, in which all information would be stored in magnetic or optical computer-readable form. Because paper documents have continued to be of integral importance in the office setting, the Xerox Corporation has recently shifted its focus onto new technologies that combine efficient uses of paper output, called **intelligent documents,** with computerized information systems. See INTELLIGENT DOCUMENT.

parachute *noun*
   (*Slang*) See MOON ROCK.

paragliding *noun*
   A variation of hang-gliding, popular in the Alps, in which a participant dons a harness attached to canopylike wings, runs down a mountain slope to gain speed, and glides into the valley below.

parallel processing *noun*
   See MASSIVELY PARALLEL PROCESSING.

parking *noun*
   See STOCK PARKING.

particle marketing *noun*
See MICRO-MARKETING.

patch *noun*
A patch worn on the skin for delivering medication transdermally. Used with *the*. See FENTANYL PATCH; NICOTINE PATCH.

pathography *noun*
A form of biography that emphasizes the negative aspects of the subject's life, such as misfortunes, scandals, failures, or substance abuse. [Coined by novelist Joyce Carol Oates]

patient rights *noun plural*
The implicit and explicit rights of a medical patient, including informed consent about treatment, the right to refuse care, assurance of privacy and confidentiality, and the right to have an effective living will.

Patriot Missile *noun*
A defensive missile widely used during the Persian Gulf War to intercept attacking Scud missiles in midair.

patrolling *noun*
(*Teenage Slang*) Aimless wandering associated with a state of indecision among a group about how to spend an evening.

pay for skills *noun*
See SKILL-BASED PAY.

payroll adjustment *noun*
The act or an instance of firing an employee. Also called **released resources; reshaping.**

PCN *noun*

A new form of cellular phone technology that provides a range of technical opportunities for improved cordless phone service as well as more efficient cable TV operations. PCNs, according to *Variety*, "could put cable in a number of promising new businesses and allow consumers to make phone calls from inexpensive cordless phones. Some analysts say PCNs could replace much of today's wired telephone service and be a source of billions of dollars of revenue for the cable industry." [Abbreviation of Personal Communications Network]

PCR *noun*

A powerful genetic research technology that is "fueling a revolution in genetic discoveries by making it possible to replicate strands of genetic material rapidly and in enormous quantities, significantly enhancing the ability of researchers to detect specific genes and segments of DNA," according to science writer Ron Winslow. [Abbreviation of Polymerase Chain Reaction]

peace dividend *noun*

Federal monies conceived as savable from the reduced defense budget during a peaceful period, as that following the end of the Cold War; especially such monies made usable to help the poor, improve health care, and fund a variety of community services.

pen computing *noun*

A computer application in which the user marks information on a page-size photosensitive tablet with a light-emitting pen-shaped instrument. Pen computing is especially useful for graphics, on-the-spot recording, and for allowing the user to write by hand rather than having to type on a keyboard.

People Like Us *noun plural*
See PLUs.

people pill *noun*
A strategy against corporate takeover in which the top executives of a proposed target company agree in advance to resign en masse if they believe the stockholders are not getting the best deal possible, or if the proposed merger will threaten the jobs of some of the executives. Also called **Pac-Man counterattack.**

performance panache *noun*
The combined qualities of power, comfort, style, and sleekness. Applied to athletic wear, sports cars, and other subjects of competitive advertising and marketing battles.

PERS *noun*
Emergency communication systems that are marketed especially to the elderly and disabled and that automatically dial and call for help with a minimum amount of user effort. "Nearly one-half million older and disabled Americans now use these devices in their homes," according to writer John Sherwood in *AARP NEWS.* [Abbreviation of Personal Emergency Response Systems]

petite sirah *noun*
See SYRAH.

PFB *noun*
A painful skin condition of the face prevalent among Black men. PFB is exacerbated by shaving, which causes sharpened facial hair bristles to curl back under the skin. These ingrown hairs act as splinters, producing inflammation, boillike infections, and scarring. [From **p**seudo**f**olliculitis **b**arbae] Also called **pseudofolliculitis barbae.**

phallocentric *adjective*
Of or relating to phallocentrism.

phallocentrism *noun*
An insistently assertive attitude exalting male interests and needs. A term originated by feminist writers.

pharm food *noun*
See NUTRICEUTICAL.

PHB *noun*
A biodegradable plastic that holds promise for environmentally sensible packaging of the future. [From **polyhy**droxy**b**utyrate]

phosphor burn-in *noun*
The unintentional and unwanted etching of images into a computer monitor, usually caused by leaving the monitor on for long periods of time without changing the image. Phosphor burn-in is a typical problem with monitors and video terminals used for games, in which sharp colored lines remain on the screen for long periods of time.

Photo CD system *noun*
A new technology from Eastman Kodak that allows a photographic image to be recorded on traditional film stock and then either developed as usual or digitized and transferred to a compact disk that can be played and viewed with a television monitor.

physician-assisted suicide *noun*
See SUICIDE MACHINE.

pickle card *noun*
A ticket for a fund-raising game popular in Nebraska that has tabs for the purchaser to pull out, a matching of the

symbols underneath making the purchaser a winner. [From the practice common in the Middle West years ago of selling such cards from empty pickle jars]

pigtail macaque (ma-KAK) *noun*
See MACACA NEMESTRINA.

Pink *noun*
The working name for a new computer operating system developed at Apple Computer and based on the linking together of small programs, or **objects,** that can share files and link data from one program to another seamlessly.

Pink Angel *noun*
A member of an unarmed anticrime street patrol, as in New York City and San Francisco, made up chiefly of gay men and lesbians and organized to protect neighborhood residents who have been victimized by bias attacks.

place-based media *noun*
An advertising strategy of placing specific commercial TV programs into designated public facilities, such as airport lounges, health facility waiting rooms, retail establishments, and classrooms.

PLAN *noun*
A movement chiefly among urban planners, governments, and residents on the West Coast that aims to avoid the many planning problems now common to Los Angeles and its suburbs. [Acronym for **P**revent **L**os **A**ngeles **N**ow]
See LOS ANGELIZATION.

play *verb*
(*Slang*) To lie to, as in, "Are you playing me about that thing?" An urban street term.

play or pay financing *noun*

A financial planning approach to employee health insurance that requires employers to provide private coverage to their workers or pay into a public plan.

plex

1. *noun* A multiscreen cinema; a multiplex, as in, "They built four plexes last year in Cincinnati." **2.** *verb* To retrofit (an older auditorium) into smaller units for viewing movies.

pluggie *noun*

A term coined by writer Laura Bergheim to describe a modern-day person whom she sees as "a creature of comfort and convenience, overstimulated by artificial intelligence and instant gratification, but underexposed to genuine experience and the virtues of patience." The term combines *yuppie* with *plug,* this group being seen as readily plugging itself into walkmans, TVs, and other passive entertainments.

PLUs (pee-el-yooz) *noun plural*

People who are members of one's own social or demographic group regarded as distinct from and superior to other groups viewed as outsiders. [Acronym for **P**eople **L**ike **Us**] Also called **People Like Us.**

plus-size woman *noun*

A newly identified market segment in the fashion industry for clothing designed for the larger woman. "Leading manufacturers of lingerie, hosiery, bodywear, activewear and jeans," according to fashion writer Diane Clehane, "are also creating lines for the size 14+ customer. Perhaps the biggest endorsement the larger size customer can get from the fashion industry is to be given her own stores and departments to shop in. There are more than 100 specialty stores catering to this new important customer."

pointless pollution *noun*
Environmental pollution exemplified by peanut-shaped styrofoam packaging pellets used in shipping that are not biodegradable.

pollution rights *noun plural*
A new legal concept, following the passage of the Clean Air Act of 1990, that allows corporations to engage in a type of market-based trading of compliance to environmental regulations. For example, Mobil Oil Corporation paid about $3 million to the city of South Gate, California, to purchase rights to emit an additional 900 pounds of noxious gas vapors each day. South Gate had acquired these rights from General Motors, which closed down a plant in that city. The economic concept behind this practice is that an overall lower level of environmental pollution can be achieved most effectively by combining financial incentives and pollution reduction at the same time.

polybag *noun*
A polyethylene plastic bag produced in a wide variety of sizes and strengths and typically used commercially for packaging written material such as appliance instructions, direct mail advertisements, or magazine **outserts** or at home for a variety of purposes ranging from packing sandwiches to bagging leaves.

po-mo *adjective, noun*
(*Informal*) Postmodern; postmodernism.

Popeye *noun*
An Israeli air-to-ground missile.

portable telephone number *noun*
See EASY REACH 700.

postnup *noun*
A financial contract between spouses that sets out a settlement in case of divorce well before the event takes place. [Shortening of *postnup*tial agreement]

posy sniffer *noun*
(*Slang*) An environmentalist.

pot sticker *noun*
A dumpling that is cooked or steamed in a pot, as in Chinese cooking.

pound *noun*
(*Slang*) A .357 handgun, a relatively heavy weapon.

POW (pee-oh-dub-uhl-yoo) *noun*
See EPW.

PowerBook *noun*
A portable Apple computer that is specifically designed to allow the user to read electronic books. "A touch of a button turns the page or allows the reader to flip back and forth. Users can dog-ear the corner of a page to mark their places, or attach an electronic paper clip for easy reference." (*Time*)

pre-woman *noun*
A female human being younger than a mature woman. A feminist and bias-free term used in preference to *girl*.

Primes *noun plural*
Trading securities that offer a hedge against sudden price declines and appreciate slightly more slowly than the indi-

vidual stocks themselves. "Traded on the American Stock Exchange, Primes function like lower-risk versions of 26 blue-chip issues. The Primes allow investors to collect almost all of the dividend income from the related stock and any appreciation in the price of the stock up to a preset maximum." (Karen Slater, *Wall Street Journal*)

privileging *noun*
Special attention and credence given to one theory, group, position, or point of view over others.

prolistics *noun*
The development of distribution strategies used especially by manufacturers introducing new products. [Said to be from *pro*curement + *logistics*]

Prop Art *noun*
Art with a strong political content; propaganda that masquerades as art. [By shortening, from *prop*aganda]

props *noun plural*
(*Slang*) The people or weapons one relies on for protection. An urban street term.

protected mode *noun*
The natural operating mode of Intel based 286, 386, and 486 computers, which allows maximum use of the hardware and permits programs to operate at their highest possible speeds. Since not all programs can handle this power, the computer can also run at a more controlled, somewhat less efficient, but highly manageable mode called the **virtual-86 mode.** See DOS EXTENDER; VIRTUAL-86 MODE.

Protein C *noun*
A protein that is necessary for the regulation of blood clotting, occurs naturally in trace amounts in humans, and

has recently been extracted from the milk of genetically engineered pigs. Protein C shows promise as an anticoagulant in treating heart disease and stroke but it has been difficult to extract and collect up until this time.

PSA *noun*
A new blood test for early diagnosis of prostate cancer. "The test, known as PSA, for prostate-specific antigen, is reshaping the diagnosis and treatment of prostate cancer, the second-leading cancer killer of men after lung cancer." (Ron Winslow, *Wall Street Journal*) [Abbreviation of Prostate-Specific Antigen]

pseudofolliculitis barbae *noun*
See PFB.

P-Star *noun*
A new equation for forecasting inflation, developed by the Federal Reserve. Derived from the classical inflation mathematics of Irving Fisher, the new method, according to economist Lacy Hunt, uses as a starting point "the same equation as Professor Fisher . . . [but] instead of using the actual real growth rate in the economy in the equation, the Federal Reserve substitutes a figure . . . which it deems to be the long-term annual potential growth rate of the economy." This change presumably allows for significantly more accurate forecasting.

pubcaster *noun*
A public broadcasting station or network.

Pump Inflatable shoe *noun*
A shoe manufactured by Reebok that provides a custom fit and additional cushioning with a built-in air pump that

automatically inflates chambers in the shoe. Also called **inflatable shoe.**

pure-play *adjective*
Of, relating to, or being a company that focuses on a single product or service and offers an efficient way to invest in that category.

PUT *noun*
A broadcasting industry measure of the percentage increase or decrease in the number of television viewers in specified demographic groups, as men between 18 and 35, or children between 8 and 11. [Acronym for **P**eople **U**sing **T**V]

Q card *noun*
A Japanese baseball card featuring the photo and statistics of a player from one of Japan's two major leagues.

QMB
Abbreviation of Qualified Medicare Beneficiaries, low-income individuals who are eligible not only for benefits, but whose premiums and deductibles are also paid by the government.

QR program *noun*
A program for distributing a new product to the market efficiently. [Shortening of **Q**uick-**R**esponse]

Q Sound *noun*

A special effects audio technology that is based on a computerized sound mixing and enhancing process. Q Sound technology has been used extensively in commercial advertising and, recently, by performers such as Bon Jovi to provide a spatial three-dimensional sound imaging that gives the effect of the music filling the entire listening area.

quats *noun plural*

Ammonium compounds used in shampoos and hair conditioners to reduce the natural static electricity that makes hair difficult to control. [Shortening of *quaternary ammonium compounds*]

quinua (KEEN-wah) *noun*

A protein-rich grain with a nutty flavor.

R

race norming *noun*

A scoring practice on standardized tests in which the actual test score is adjusted up or down to reflect the relative ranking of the person being tested within his or her race's test norms.

radical *adjective*

(*Teenage Slang*) Amazingly impressive or different, as in, "Really radical hair."

radical dude *noun*

See DUDICAL.

rainmaker *noun*

An aggressive and creative developer of business. "Asked if that makes him a rainmaker, Kelly said: 'All of us are that. Nobody's just a rainmaker. He's going to be developing client relationships.' " (*Los Angeles Times*)

Ralph *interjection*
Used to suggest the sound of vomiting. Chiefly a college student use.

rapoush (rah-POOSH) *noun*
A loose-fitting, solid-colored garment that fastens up the front and is worn by Iranian women.

RAS protein *noun*
A biochemical substance central to the process of cholesterol formation and present in the gene that triggers certain kinds of cancers, such as pancreatic cancer and colon cancer.

Rational Recovery *noun*
An alcoholism treatment program that is an alternative to the Twelve Steps program of Alcoholics Anonymous and focuses on rational choice, willpower, individual decision-making, and behavioral change.

raw art *noun*
See OUTSIDER ART.

RBRVS *noun*
A system designed to establish payments to physicians based on the importance, necessity, and difficulty of the procedures they perform. [Abbreviation of Resource Based Relative Value Scale] Also called **resource based payment.**

RDI *noun*
A new standard for nutrition that replaces the current RDA (recommended daily allowance) figures used to sug-

gest adequate levels of vitamin and mineral intake. [Abbreviation of Reference Daily Intake]

read-after-write *noun*
A new computer technology that allows data to be reviewed as it is being recorded on backup tape, allowing a higher level of quality assurance than previously possible.

readeo *noun*
A new publishing practice in which a book and companion videocassette are packaged and sold together.

reality check *noun*
A clear-headed assessment of one's circumstances especially to determine if one has been engaging in wishful thinking.

reality programming *noun*
A category of television broadcasting that concentrates on showing real people in unrehearsed real events or realistic reenactments. See ON-SCENE SHOW; REALITY SHOW.

reality show *noun*
A television program featuring real people and events videotaped as they are happening. Subjects range from marital battles, family feuds, and the crises of everyday life to police actions and emergency squads at accident scenes.

rebirthing *noun*
A therapeutic practice for stress reduction and self-awareness based on a technique developed by Leonard Orr called **conscious connected breathing.** Rebirthing allegedly enables the participant to achieve an awareness of mind, body, perception, the emotions, and the influence of

others by overcoming past traumatic events deeply buried in the unconscious mind.

re-career *noun*
A second career, usually one embarked upon by an older person in preference to retirement.

recombinoid *noun*
A toy that revives the form of an earlier toy that has lost popularity and combines it with the form of a currently popular toy or other product, benefiting from the established name identification of the older toy and the existing interest in the current product. For example, Mattel's Food Fighters Junk-Food Army combines the older Fun With Food and the G.I. Joe toys.

rectenna *noun*
A proposed flat disk antenna, about 65 feet in diameter, to be used on the Endosat experimental aircraft for receiving low-frequency microwave beams as a source of power for the pilotless high-altitude aircraft. [From *rect*ifying an*tenna*] See CONDOR; ENDOSAT.

redshirting *noun*
A practice on the part of parents of delaying a child's enrollment in kindergarten in order to allow the child more nonschool experience with playmates and more physical and emotional development before entering school. [From *redshirting*, a practice in sports of benching a player for a season in order to use the player's eligibility in a following year]

red zone *noun*
The part of a football playing field within an opponent's 20-yard line.

referent power *noun*
A psychological technique used in marketing and advertising that attempts to bring about group conformity by urging emulation of the behavior of an admired group to change the behavior of a targeted group. For example, through the use of referent power, successful athletes may be held up to inner city adolescents to emulate in order to encourage more productive behavior patterns or to urge the purchase of one type of product over another.

reg-neg *noun*
A process in which interested parties can negotiate changes in federal regulatory practices. For example, oil companies can negotiate changes to environmental regulations affecting refineries. [From *reg*ulatory *neg*otiation]

relationship marketing *noun*
A principle in advertising and magazine publishing that long-term loyal readers of a publication are more reliable prospects for advertisers than larger numbers of readers who may have been lured to the publication through subscription incentives.

relationship selling *noun*
Selling through a closed informal industry network of potential buyers who know one another, exchange information, and generally favor purchasing from sellers involved in the network.

released resources *noun*
See PAYROLL ADJUSTMENT.

repetitive strain injury *noun*
A painful occupational disability, as of the wrist, caused by continued repetitive physical actions, such as computer

keyboarding, soldering, threading machine needles, or playing certain musical instruments. Also called **RSI**.

rephotography *noun*
A postmodern style in art photography pioneered by Richard Prince in 1977. A kind of **appropriation art,** it consists of photographing photographs "to isolate gestures, postures and logos, primarily from magazine advertisements, representing them with little alteration as large-scale photographic prints." (Whitney Museum Calendar brochure)

rescue *verb*
To use protest as a means of interfering with the aborting of (a fetus). [From the activities of the anti-abortion group Operation Rescue]

reshaping *noun*
See PAYROLL ADJUSTMENT.

Resolution Trust Corporation *noun*
See R.T.C.

resource based payment *noun*
See RBRVS.

reverse mortgage *noun*
A mortgage loan made to a homeowner by a bank in monthly installments up to the full value of the home or in one lump sum requiring no payments until the house is sold or the owner dies. While the bank receives full equity in the home, the homeowner receives cash for living expenses. These instruments are used primarily by retirees who do not wish to sell their homes while they are still living in them, but could use the cash value of their homes

during these same years. Also called **reverse-equity mortgage.**

right *interjection*
Used to express ironic disagreement or doubt, as in the exchange, "I'm really going to beat you this time." "Right. Now pick up your racquet and let's play."

Ring of Fire *noun*
An area encircling the Pacific Ocean known for its frequent earthquakes.

rising-rate CD *noun*
A certificate of deposit that pays progressively higher predetermined rates every three to six months over the life of the certificate. See BUMP CD.

Rita *noun*
The new name for the former official Soviet press agency Tass. [Acronym for **R**ussian **I**nformation **T**elegraph **A**gency]

roadblock *noun*
An advertising technique using a precision-timed saturation campaign, or **blitz,** in which television commercials for a product are run at the same time on all major stations. The roadblock is viewed as an economical way of getting blanket coverage, especially for a new product, since its simultaneity assures that viewers cannot avoid seeing it.

roadkill *noun*
A dead animal that has been killed by a passing vehicle and left along the roadway.

Rollerblade *noun*
A brand of in-line roller skate manufactured by Rollerblade, Inc. of Minnetonka, Minnesota.

roll-up *noun*

A financial device in which a large, publicly traded investing unit is created from the funds of several smaller nontraded limited partnerships. The roll-up is intended to provide economy of scale and easy liquidity, but it has created controversy as to whether it is more beneficial to the general partners than it is to the investors in the smaller entities.

Rose Garden strategy *noun*

A presidential campaign strategy in which the incumbent president is set apart from opponents as the person who is fully informed and in control of the nation's destiny and whose policies are based on realities that other candidates can't fully understand. "[The Rose Garden strategy] always has one aim: to lift [the president's] political fortunes by wrapping him in the trappings of his office and having him take steps to demonstrate . . . that he is the man in charge and others are just wannabes." (Andrew Rosenthal) [Named after the White House rose garden, famous as a site for presidential news conferences]

Rotisserie League *noun*

A multi-player game in which participants manage imaginary baseball teams and leagues according to accepted rules. The games and transactions may be conducted over computer networks, telephone lines, and by mail, and several magazines and newsletters inform fans worldwide of the latest standings. "Rotisserie League, for those of you in the baseball dark ages, is sometimes called Fantasy Baseball. The game has swept the nation — *USA Today* estimates that 750,000 people now play it — and I'm proud to say I'm one of the cofounders of the original league." (Peter Gethers) [Named for its origin at the now-defunct Rotisserie restaurant in Manhattan] Also called **Fantasy Baseball.**

Royal Free disease *noun*
See CHRONIC FATIGUE SYNDROME.

RSI *noun*
See REPETITIVE STRAIN INJURY.

R.T.C. *noun*
The Resolution Trust Corporation, a federal agency that oversees the bailout of the savings and loan industry. Following the S&L crisis of recent years, Congress has had to appropriate large amounts of money to keep the R.T.C. solvent.

Rubbergate *noun*
The scandal involving overdraft abuses of the now defunct House Bank, which served members of Congress and their families. Hundreds of lawmakers were cited as regularly bouncing checks or writing checks before their salaries were deposited at the bank. Although it was claimed that this was standard operating procedure for the bank, and technically not illegal, it led to the downfall of several members of Congress as the public responded negatively to these fiduciary peccadilloes.

RU 486 *noun*
A pharmaceutical product invented in France that prevents a fertilized egg from developing into a fetus. Used as a postcoital birth control method, it is intended to be taken during the first seven weeks of pregnancy. Also called **abortion pill; French abortion pill; morning-after pill.**

Rybinsk (RIB-uhnsk, RIB-uhntsk) *noun*
The Russian city formerly known as Andropov.

S
....

sabermetrics *noun*
  The science of baseball statistics. [From *SABR*, acronym for the **S**ociety of **A**merican **B**aseball **R**esearch]

Sachs Plan *noun*
  An economic plan developed by economist Jeffrey Sachs and designed to allow a formerly communist country to switch to a free market economy in the shortest possible time. Also called **shock therapy.**

SAD *noun*
  See WINTER BLUES. [Acronym for **S**easonal **A**ffective **D**isorder]

Safe Ears *noun*
  See CONDOM EARRING.

St. Petersburg *noun*
  The Russian city formerly known as Leningrad (previously called St. Petersburg).

sampling *noun*
  The process by which small segments of sound from another performer's recording are included in the recording of a new piece of music, often in the background. Sampling may be done by digital technologies, which can change the original sound in numerous ways, or by merely snipping sections of tape from different performers and splicing them together without modification.

sand rights *noun*

A new legal theory that holds that individuals who benefit from building projects that take sand from beaches, prevent its replenishment, or erode the beach line should be responsible for the loss and pay for damage or restoration to the beach. "The theory holds that beaches have a 'right' to the sand that would naturally flow to them and that the states have a right to make sure they get it, even if that means that some property owners have to pay to make it happen." (*New York Times*)

SAP *noun*

A television broadcast sideband, outside the ordinary frequency range, that transmits a special audio program accessible to viewers with a decoder commonly found in stereo television sets and in hi-fi VCRs. In addition to its use for stereo reception, SAP has become especially popular for simultaneous bilingual programming, in which an English-broadcast show can carry the Spanish-language equivalent for simultaneous transmission. [Acronym for **S**econdary **A**udio **P**rogramming]

sapote (suh-POH-tay) *noun*

See MAMEY.

satisficing *noun*

A business practice of factoring price or performance data over many markets, regions, or groups in order to achieve a balanced whole or an accurate total picture of a product's performance.

SAT-I *noun*

A Scholastic Aptitude Test revision for testing verbal skills, mathematics, and reasoning ability.

SAT-II *noun*

A Scholastic Achievement Test revision for testing performance and ability in specific subject areas, such as foreign languages, chemistry, or history.

SBS *noun*

See SICK BUILDING SYNDROME.

ScanFone *noun*

A service recently introduced by Bell Atlantic that consists of a standard touch-tone telephone keypad and a magnetic credit card reader by means of which a subscriber can shop at home and charge purchases on a credit card.

scanning tunneling microscope *noun*

See STM.

schwing *interjection*

(*Slang*) Used on the TV sketch and film *Wayne's World* to express appreciation of a woman the characters find attractive.

scoop *verb*

(*Slang*) to watch (someone passing by), especially in an admiring way.

scripting *noun*

A technique in personal computing that allows a user to instruct the computer ahead of time to perform a variety of different tasks when the user is not present, either at a certain specific time or under a certain condition.

Scud missile *noun*

A somewhat unsophisticated missile used in launchings by the Iraqis during the Persian Gulf War. The name was originally derived from the SS-1A Scunner missile used by Germany at the end of World War II.

scum rock *noun*
Rock music characterized by features of heavy metal, bluegrass, and old-fashioned rock and roll and having lyrics expressing working-class attitudes.

scuttling *noun*
The removal of one person's pants by another in a public or semi-public place, usually in a partying atmosphere, according to Helen Gurley Brown of *Cosmopolitan* magazine. Also called **depantsing.**

sea-gull model *noun*
(*Slang*) An unsatisfactory consultant in business who makes a brief appearance to present ideas, follows up with minimum visits to outline strategy, and then vanishes.

sealeg *noun*
Imitation shellfish meat that is shaped and colored like an Alaskan crab claw and is made from shredded fish, mostly pollack. It is used in seafood salads, in sushi, and as a topping for pizza or other dishes.

seasonal affective disorder *noun*
See WINTER BLUES.

seasonal depression *noun*
See WINTER BLUES.

sell-through tape *noun*
A low-priced newly released videotape that is designed to encourage purchase rather than rental in video stores. Particularly effective with family fare, such as Disney's *Beauty and the Beast*, these sell-through tapes include many very inexpensive cartoon classics, as well as some older black-and-white film classics that are attractive to videophiles.

sensitivity analysis *noun*
  A statistical technique in which a change in one variable is compared with changes in other variables to determine which is more likely to be cause and which to be effect.

Serbia *noun*
  A former republic of Yugoslavia that formed the Federal Republic of Yugoslavia with Montenegro in April 1992.

serve *verb*
  (*Slang*) To dominate. The new meaning has caused a controversy in Los Angeles, where the police credo that is emblazoned on all police cars is 'To protect and to serve,' a usage found offensive by those who have become familiar with the new meaning.

777 *noun*
  The new Boeing 777 airliner, scheduled for delivery in 1995.

sex worker *noun*
  A prostitute. A feminist term.

shade *verb*
  (*Slang*) To subject (a competitor or critic) to verbal abuse, criticism, or scorn; throw shade. An urban street term.

shadow lobbyist *noun*
  See SHADOW SENATOR.

shadow senator *noun*
  The political position of the elected representative from the District of Columbia to the United States Senate. Because the post is not recognized by Congress, does not carry a congressional vote, and does not qualify for public election law funding it is regarded as a shadow rather than real

elected position. Jesse Jackson was the first to hold this position.

Sharypovo (shahr-ee-PO-vo) *noun*
The Russian city formerly known as Chernenko.

Sheilaism *noun*
An individualistic, nondogmatic, often unaffiliated outlook on religious matters. [Coined by Robert N. Bellah in his book *Habits of the Heart*]

Shelby knot *noun*
A new necktie knot resembling the reverse half-Windsor, which has been popular since the beginning of this century. [Named after Minneapolis newscaster Don Shelby]

shell company *noun*
A defunct public company that can use its stock to acquire a small operating company. "The owners of the operating company," according to financial writer Floyd Norris, "effectively give up a part of their company's equity to the owners of the shell to get a public listing. Such companies are thereby able to go public without having prospectuses reviewed by the staff of the Securities and Exchange Commission," a major practical benefit in terms of efficacy and a significant financial savings in terms of legal fees.

Shelter-Pak *noun*
A hooded, full-length waterproof overcoat that can double as a sleeping bag, designed for homeless people by students at the Philadelphia College of Textiles and Science.

shepherding *noun*
A practice in some fundamentalist sects and communal religious groups of encouraging or requiring members to follow the teachings, advice, and directives of their leaders about decisions involving family, jobs, education, choice of

partner, housing, personal relationships, and many other personal matters.

shermed *noun*
(*Slang*) High on angel dust. An urban street term.

shocked quartz *noun*
Shattered quartz crystals created by intense heat and pressure, as those recently found in shale dating back over 200 million years and suggestive of the possibility that they were formed when a large meteorite collided with earth around that time. See KILLER ASTEROID.

shock therapy *noun*
The attempt on the part of a formerly communist country to establish a new economic order rapidly, following its transition to capitalism. "Shock therapy usually includes immediate convertibility of a country's currency, the privatization of state enterprises and introduction of market pricing. The initial impact falls heavily on the workers through higher prices, widespread unemployment and lower living standards." (*Los Angeles Times*) See SACHS PLAN.

shock treatment *noun*
A crash program of free-market reforms designed to stir an economy into action, such as that instituted by President Boris Yeltsin's government following the dissolution of the Soviet Union.

shoegazers *noun plural*
Musical groups alleged to be "looking toe-wards during performances [and] concentrating more on creating their hazy waves of guitar wash than bothering with any mid-song, audience-geared pleasantries," according to music critic Alex Smith.

shottie *noun*
(*Slang*) A shotgun. An urban street term.

shoulder surfer *noun*
A person who illegally acquires and later uses or sells someone's telephone credit card number by surreptitiously watching as the caller punches in the number on a public phone or eavesdropping as the caller recites the number to an operator.

show time *noun*
(*Slang*) A point in a sports event when players dazzle fans by showing off their athletic virtuosity.

shreddin' *noun*
See FOOTBAG.

shusa *noun*
A Japanese term for a team leader, especially one in a factory or business setting.

sick building syndrome *noun*
A constellation of persistent and unexplainable symptoms, such as eye or skin irritation, sore throat, headache, nausea, and dizziness, associated with an office building that may be environmentally polluted. Although no specific cause has been identified, likely sources of sick building syndrome may be indoor pollution spread through the ventilating system or high levels of dust and chemical contaminants in the walls, floors, or in the building structure itself. Also called **SBS**.

signifying *noun*
A form of chanting native to African-American culture, characterized by a rhythmically delivered and often rhym-

ing form of teasing, insult, or jest. Rap is a contemporary form of signifying.

silent depression *noun*
The ongoing recession and depressionlike effects that with some fluctuations have been a constant strain on the US economy since the end of the Vietnam War.

simplified fare *noun*
A fare structure in the airline industry that seeks to reduce some airfares and to arrive at uniform fare levels between travel points with a minimum of exceptions and restrictions.

single-payer system *noun*
A proposed health insurance system in which everyone would be covered by one publicly financed insurance program and the government would serve as the sole insurer for health care services.

sjamboks *noun*
A hard rubber whip three feet in length that was formerly used by police in South Africa to control protesters in local demonstrations. Its use was banned in 1989 over concerns about the image it created internationally.

skeleton *noun*
A small sled used for racing down an icy track head first. The world's foremost skeleton track is the Cresta Run, in St. Moritz, Switzerland.

skid-bid *noun*
(*Slang*) Time served in prison.

skill-based pay *noun*
A method of paying employees for the specific knowledge, skills, and abilities they bring to their jobs rather than

for the number of people they supervise, their managerial title, or their years in service. According to the *New York Times*, this system is being used at Salomon Brothers, whose new pay plan "will reflect an employee's specific job skills and a team's success in achieving performance goals that they have hammered out with their customers." Also called **knowledge-based compensation; pay for skills.**

skim pricing *noun*
   The practice of charging the highest price consumers are likely to pay for a new product when it is introduced.

skin game *noun*
   A golf competition in which the total prize, or **skin,** is apportioned on a per-hole basis, with the requirement for payout that one player alone has the lowest score on a given hole.

skronk *noun*
   A genre of music originating in New York's Lower East Side during the early 1980s that includes noise rock and downtown improvisation, experimental forms attempting new instrumentation and compositional techniques. See DOWNTOWN IMPROVISATION; NOISE ROCK.

slab *verb*
   To grade and hermetically seal collector-quality coins in plastic holders. "[The West Coast dealer's Professional Coin Service] now slabs 70,000 to 90,000 coins a month." (Mark Hendricks, *New York Times*)

slab *noun*
   (*Slang*) A coin that is hermetically sealed in a plastic holder, certified for quality, and tradable sight unseen on the American Numismatic Exchange.

slamming *noun*
Slam dancing, a violent dance-floor activity in which dancers deliberately slam into each other.

slap-bracelet *noun*
An inexpensive, flexible metal-slat and fabric-covered bracelet, usually brightly colored, that curls around the wrist or ankle following a downward slapping action. Favored by pre-teens and adolescents, slap-bracelets are banned in some schools where the slapping activity becomes more dominant than the wearing of the bracelets themselves.

Slapp *noun*
A lawsuit that is pressed by a well-funded plaintiff, is generally viewed as an attempt at intimidation, and is typically filed against social activists, environmentalists, disgruntled consumers, or people protesting real estate development projects. The *Wall Street Journal* reported that Ralph Nader "is establishing a coalition dedicated to funding free counsel for people who are hit with Slapps." [Acronym for **S**trategic **L**awsuits **A**gainst **P**ublic **P**articipation]

slasher video *noun*
Videotapes of movies that feature violence, such as *Friday the 13th* and *The Texas Chain Saw Massacre*. See ANTI-SLASHER LAW.

slimer *noun*
A worker who cleans salmon by scraping away the detritus, cutting off the bad parts, and preparing it for further processing.

slime suit *noun*
A lycra-based swimsuit saturated with a water-soluble gel-like substance that makes the fabric especially slippery

when it is wet, allowing the swimmer to move faster through the water.

SLORC *noun*
The 19-member military junta that rules Myanmar (formerly Burma) with brutally repressive tactics. [Acronym for **S**tate **L**aw and **O**rder **R**estoration **C**ouncil]

Slovenia *noun*
A former republic of Yugoslavia that declared its independence in June 1991.

smart car *noun*
A car with a computer that informs the driver of the car's current location and provides suggested routes to the intended destination. The smart car "has a small video screen in the dashboard with a map showing where you are and how to get where you are heading. It also has a computer voice that tells you when a turn is coming up, a two-way radio for assistance and a cellular phone." (*New York Times*)

smart drugs *noun plural*
A class of nonprescription over-the-counter preparations, usually powders or pills, that are claimed to enhance intelligence, increase alertness, and heighten one's energy level. Usually made up of nutrients and amino-acid protein-rich substances mixed with fruit juices, these products have generally been discredited over the past several years by experts and by the FDA as ineffective for the claim made for them. Also called **smart drinks.**

smart window *noun*
A window made from special materials that let the sun in and prevent heat from escaping. Efficient models have proven capable of allowing a house to stay warm in winter

without any additional heating, thus providing a significant savings of fossil fuel and an equally significant decrease in environmental contaminants. Also called **electrochromic window.**

smashmouth basketball *noun*
   A rough-and-ready type of basketball in which player collisions, hotly contested decisions, and an overly aggressive playing style predominate.

smog exchange *noun*
   An exchange in California composed of 2,800 companies and intended to allow the member companies to trade in earned pollution allowances, which gives them financial incentives to meet clean-air goals, in preference to ordered compliance through specific regulations. See POLLUTION RIGHTS.

smog-free pump *noun*
   An environmentally safe reusable pump that is a cross between the hand pump used in window cleaning products and the aerosol pump that has proven damaging to the environment. Developed in Sweden, the smog-free pump works by ordinary air pressure created by the user's initial plunging, retaining the pressure by forcing a fluid through a tube that leads to a nozzle.

smog futures *noun*
   A new futures contract that is based on federally regulated sulphur-dioxide emissions allowances and approved by the Commodity Trading Commission for trading on the Chicago Board of Trade. These futures are based on the Clean Air Act's provision to allow utilities to trade unused portions of their allocated one-ton smog allowance.

SMSA *noun*

A region designated by the US Census Bureau having at least a central city population of over 50,000, an especially useful designation for defining target market populations. [Abbreviation for Standard Metropolitan Statistical Area]

snake-check *verb*

To anticipate expected results and avoid unintended consequences by closely examining from different points of view all the implications of a plan in advance of its implementation.

snap *verb*

(*Slang*) To criticize; put down; diss. An urban street term.

snap diva *noun*

(*Slang*) A Black male who shows disdain with a highly stylized choreography of finger-snapping, as depicted in the documentary film *Tongues Untied*. A gay urban street term.

snapshot accounting *noun*

A business-evaluation principle that the true value of a company on a given day can be determined specifically and often differs from its overall value as calculated by more traditional means. For example, in the natural gas—producing industry, ceiling write-downs are required to provide what is, in effect, a snapshot of a utility's true worth at the moment. See CEILING TEST.

snipe *verb*

To paste up advertising posters in a place open to public view, as on a utility pole or subway wall.

sniper *noun*

A person who snipes.

snowboard *noun*

A board that incorporates features of a ski, a skateboard, and a surfboard and is used in snowboarding.

snowboarding *noun*
A sport in which the rider's feet are strapped to a single board whose motion is controlled by the rider's twisting the body or by the application of pressure to the edge of the board by distributing body weight in different areas.

soccer ball molecule *noun*
An oddly shaped molecule consisting of eight titanium atoms and 12 carbon atoms symmetrically arranged in a 12-sided cage resembling a soccer ball. Dr. Welford Castleman, one of its discoverers, believes the molecule "is likely to have unique electrical and chemical properties that might find important uses in computer information storage and pollution control."

sochu (soh-CHOO) *noun*
A distilled spirit similar to whiskey and popular in Japan.

social marketing *noun*
A new branch of commercial marketing designed to change public attitudes and behaviors with regard to public issues, such as smoking and alcohol use, drug abuse, education, the environment, AIDS, or the use of nuclear energy. See DEMARKETING.

soft money *noun*
Money contributed to a political campaign that is outside the restrictions imposed by the Federal Election Commission on national campaigns. This would include money that appears to support the voting process rather than a specific candidate or party, while its actual use might be to increase local voting or shed light on local issues beneficial to a specific candidate.

sokaiya (so-KI-yah)
A Japanese term for disruptive, scheming stockholders who are often tied to criminal groups and demand payoffs and protection money to keep quiet at stockholder meetings.

Solar Alpha clothing *noun*
    Cold weather clothing made from a solar efficient fabric permeated with zirconium carbonide. The synthetic fabric rapidly absorbs the sun's heat and at the same time efficiently retains the heat of the body inside the clothing.

Solidarismo (sol-ee-dar-EES-moh) *noun*
    A Latin American alternative to traditional unionism, an employee-inspired movement that recognizes the functional interdependence between management and labor and stresses employee stock ownership, voluntary membership, and participatory decision-making in many areas of a company's activities.

Son of Sam law *noun*
    A New York law enacted to prevent criminals from profiting by telling their stories in books or movies and unanimously struck down by the US Supreme Court on December 10, 1991. "The high court ruled that the so-called Son of Sam law, named after a serial killer whose 1977 murders inspired the statute, violated the First Amendment's guarantee of free speech." (Paul M. Barrett, *Wall Street Journal*)

S.O.S. *noun*
    A technical support service provided by computer companies in which CD-ROM disks are given to the customer to provide on-the-spot technical support for business software systems and applications. [Abbreviation of Support On Site]

sound bite *verb*
    To condense and simplify (an issue) for a convenient fit into a brief TV or radio spot or segment.

soy ink *noun*
    An environmentally safe printing ink derived from soybeans. Advantages of this ink over the traditional volatile

chemical inks include its permanence, ease of cleaning, and freedom from environmental contamination both in manufacturing and use.

spectrum *noun*
A range of electromagnetic waves that is designated by the Federal Communications Commission to serve as a broadcasting airwave for sending signals for radio, television, and cellular telephone transmissions.

speedball *noun*
(*Slang*) See MOON ROCK.

speed metal *noun*
A fast, loud, and raucous form of heavy metal music. See GLAM; METAL FUNK; THRASH.

spend down *noun*
The process by which individuals must reduce their assets and income to the low levels that will enable them to qualify for Medicaid.

spew *verb*
(*Teenage Slang*) To vomit.

spiedie (SPEE-dee) *noun*
Marinated chunks of meat grilled on a skewer and served on a slice of Italian bread. A dining specialty in Binghamton, New York.

splatterpunk *noun*
A genre of popular fiction in which violence is described in lurid detail.

spooged *adjective*
(Of a hairstyle popular among teenagers) Sticking straight up or out to the sides.

sport climbing *noun*
A sport resembling mountain climbing whereby the participant scales human-made vertical walls, called **climbing walls** or **treadwalls,** with adjustable footholds and handholds allowing a wide and controlled variation of level of difficulty. See CLIMBING GYM.

sports bottle *noun*
A plastic bottle with a watertight snap top or screw-on lid that contains a snugly fitted flexible straw and cap designed to prevent leakage and allow drinking for the jogger, athlete, driver, or other person on the move. Also called **squeeze bottle.**

sports drink *noun*
Any of various noncarbonated drinks asserted to boost energy and replenish water in the body. Brands such as Gatorade and PowerAde, originally marketed for athletes, have found wide acceptance with a health- and exercise-conscious public.

sprout *noun*
Any of the people, constituting about one-quarter of the population, who display both positive and negative opinions on environmental issues and are yet not fully prepared to finance measures to improve the environment. [From an environmental study done by the Roper Organization]

squeal rule *noun*
A controversial federal regulation requiring federally funded family planning clinics to notify the parents of pa-

tients under 18 years of age that the patients are seeking prescription contraceptives.

squeegee people *noun*
(*Slang*) People in large cities who approach drivers of cars stopped at traffic lights or caught in gridlock and aggressively offer to clean their windshields, typically with a squeegee or a rag.

squeeze bottle *noun*
See SPORTS BOTTLE.

squib kick *noun*
A football play in which the ball is kicked to the opposing team low and on the ground, making it difficult to receive, in the hope that the ball will be fumbled by a defensive lineman and recovered by the kicking team.

SRAMS *noun*
A new generation of computer chips that can perform calculations trillions of times per second. [Acronym for ultra-fast **s**tatic **r**andom **a**ccess **m**emory chip**s**]

SRO hotel *noun*
A usually old and converted hotel or rooming house in which most of the residents are poor and on public assistance. [Abbreviation of Single Room Occupancy hotel]

Stalingrad *adjective*
(*Slang*) Being snowed under with paperwork due for college classes.

STAR *noun*
A US missile used in the Persian Gulf War.

stay behind *noun*
A member of a group, often linked by informal networks, who was originally part of a post–World War II intelligence

program organized by the Central Intelligence Agency to combat Communism in Europe and who now continues, without official authorization or sanction, to accrue arms and conduct paramilitary operations.

Stealth bomber *noun*
The B-2 bomber, a military plane designed to elude radar detection by a variety of electronic methods and by being sheathed in radar-absorbing materials.

steel collar worker *noun*
(*Slang*) An industrial robot.

Stellar *noun*
A fat substitute derived from corn and used in salad dressings, soups, and baked goods.

Stendahl syndrome *noun*
A psychiatric condition in which a person imagines that he or she is a famous literary figure, and may even assume behaviors and characteristics associated with that figure. See JERUSALEM SYNDROME.

step aerobics *noun*
An exercise in which a small plastic platform is used for imitating the action of climbing stairs.

stereo lithography *noun*
A new computer technology that allows designers and engineers working on new products or product design modifications to build accurate computerized three-dimensional models that look and behave like the real thing, without the need for full-scale mockups.

sticker shock *noun*
The surprise experienced by a potential car buyer at the high cost of a vehicle that formerly sold for notably less.

still-image camera *noun*
   An electronic imaging camera in which the still picture is recorded on a small magnetic floppy disk and can be simultaneously displayed on a television or a video monitor.

Stinger *noun*
   An American shoulder-launched rocket capable of shooting down helicopters and low-flying aircraft. Also called **Stinger missile.**

stink *adjective*
   (*Slang*) Fine; great, as in, "I like those real stink clothes." An urban street term.

STM *noun*
   An instrument with a metallic tip only a few atoms wide. Electrons can traverse the gap between the tip and the surface, a phenomenon known as tunneling, thereby generating a tiny current that can be used to move atoms and molecules around very precisely. "Even now it is not difficult to imagine that STMs might be employed by the semiconductor industry to produce minuscule electronic devices." (J. Madeleine Nash, *Time*) [Abbreviation for Scanning Tunneling Microscope]

stock basket *noun*
   See BASKET.

stockout cost *noun*
   Losses incurred when a manufacturer, distributor, or retailer lacks the necessary inventory to fill orders.

stock parking *noun*
   A financial maneuver in which the true ownership of a stock is concealed by having one investor purchase it and

hold it under his or her name until receiving a direction to sell from the real owner who financed the undertaking. Also called **parking.**

stolen products *noun plural*
Products, such as eggs, wool, milk, and honey, taken from animals by humans. A term in animal rights activism.

stoner *noun*
(*Teenage Slang*) A delinquent or rebellious youth.

stove-top *verb*
To cook (food) in a conventional oven or on a burner rather than in a microwave oven.

strack *verb*
(*Slang*) To become mentally prepared for going into battle.

strand board *noun*
See ORIENTED STRAND BOARD.

strapped *adjective*
(*Slang*) Armed with a gun, as in, "He was strapped when he went to meet them." An urban street term.

stub stock *noun*
A publicly traded stock that because of poor business circumstances is worth significantly less than its original market value.

stuff *noun*
(*Informal*) Various fringe benefits, as free legal or investment advice, subsidized cafeterias, seminars and training programs, and discretionary days off, that are sometimes part of an employment package.

suck face *verb*
(*Slang*) To kiss passionately.

suicide machine *noun*
A machine, invented by Dr. Jack Kevorkian, that assists a person in committing suicide. Designed to help the terminally ill who feel unable or unwilling to continue to fight the illness, the controversial suicide machine allows the user, under the observation but without the direct participation of a physician (**physician-assisted suicide**), to inject a fatal drug dose intravenously. The typical machine contains a chamber holding a lethal mixture of IV-administered drugs, tubing for delivery, a hypodermic needle, and a regulator button that the user presses to release the toxic chemicals into the blood, causing instantaneous death.

sunk cost *noun*
A cost incurred in the past that should not affect future income projections or decision-making.

sun people *noun plural*
See ICE PEOPLE.

Super G *noun*
A skiing event specially designed for easy television coverage in which speed and sharp turning ability are required on a slope that is shorter than a downhill run but longer than a slalom run.

supergun *noun*
A powerful and immense cannon capable of hurling a barrage of chemical, biological, or nuclear warheads hundreds of miles. Two of these superguns were found in Iraq, apparently unused, following its defeat in the Persian Gulf

War. They were dismantled by a special UN inspection team.

superstation *noun*
A television station that in addition to serving as a local broadcast station can also reach a large national audience through cable systems. The most notable example is TBS, the Turner Broadcasting System in Atlanta.

suppress assets *verb*
To destroy sites containing antiaircraft and other weaponry. A military term.

Surfspeak *noun*
The terminology and slang used by surfers, compiled in *Surf'inary*, a dictionary written by linguist and surfer Trevor Cralle.

sweat *verb*
(*Teenage Slang*) To bother (someone); hassle.

synthetic CD4 *noun*
A synthetic drug that acts as a decoy to lure a virus away from the body's immune cells, leaving it to drift harmlessly in the bloodstream.

synthetic floater *noun*
A money fund whose investments are based on subtle changes in interest rates in the short-term municipal bond market.

syrah *noun*
A variety of grape, native to France but now grown in California, that is often confused with the **petite sirah,** which is technically a durif grape. Both varieties are used in the production of California wines.

T

. . . .

TAB
Acronym for **T**emporarily **A**ble-**B**odied.

table dancing *noun*
Topless or nude dancing in which a dancer dances on a customer's table in exchange for a tip.

tabloid TV *noun*
Sensationalistic or lurid television programs, including some talk shows and reenactments of crimes and accidents, that mimic the tone and content of tabloid newspapers. Also called **grunt shows; trash TV**. See OUTTAKE SHOW.

tacrine *noun*
See THA.

TAFY *noun*
A family whose home contains considerable electronic equipment and especially a computer. [Acronym for **t**echnically **a**dvanced **f**amily]

tagger *noun*
(*Slang*) One who vandalizes property with graffiti.

take *noun*
1. Point of view; perspective, as in, "That was a feminist's take on the situation." **2.** Interpretation; understanding, as in, "What is your take on his speech?"

take-no-prisoners *adjective*
Highly determined and uncompromising, as in, "Mr. Perot's iconoclastic, take-no-prisoners persona." (*New York Times*)

talking aisle *noun*
An aisle in a supermarket that is equipped with computerized voices programmed to give information about products and other matters to shoppers.

tambo-bambo band *noun*
A Caribbean band whose players produce music by striking bamboo rods of differing lengths and thicknesses on the ground to create a wide range of pitches and sonorities.

tamoxifen (ta-MOK-si-fen) *noun*
A drug used in hormonal therapy to block the production of estrogens that can stimulate tumor growth.

Tangent *noun*
A joint venture by IBM and Apple Computer based on the Pink operating system for designing desktop software that will allow a computer user with little or no training to perform a variety of common functions, such as scheduling, filing, and writing memos, on a computer screen that resembles an ordinary desk top. See PINK.

tanning badge *noun*
A photosensitive badge, similar to one worn by an x-ray technician, that indicates when the safe levels of exposure to sunlight have been reached or exceeded. Sunbathers, athletes, and outdoor workers are among the intended users.

tasting menu *noun*
See MENU DE DÉGUSTATION.

taxol (TAK-sawl) *noun*
A rare cancer-fighting drug extracted from the Pacific Yew tree, an endangered species. Controversy has arisen

about how many trees should be sacrificed for the sake of cancer patients whose lives might be saved through taxol administration.

techno music *noun*
   A minimalist form of electronic dance music combining elementary lyrics, industrial and machine sounds, flowing rhythms, and an array of repetitive elements subjected to synthesizer technology.

TED *noun*
   A metal or nylon grid that is inserted into the trawl cone of a shrimp net to allow sea turtles that have been accidently trapped in the net to escape. [Acronym for **T**urtle **E**xcluder **D**evice] Also called **turtle excluder device.**

telco *noun*
   Telephone company.

telemedia *noun*
   The industry that has formed around the use of 900 telephone numbers, through which callers are charged higher than normal usage charges per minute to receive various services over the phone.

telemedicine *noun*
   Electronic medical diagnosis and consultation in which patient information is transmitted over normal phone lines and by satellite by means of video and computer technologies.

teleoperator *noun*
   A robotic device that allows an operator to work a machine from a distance, especially in dealing with a dangerous industrial, military, or police problem. For example, a teleoperator can control a bomb-disabling machine from a

distance by using a helmet that simulates being next to the bomb that is being dismantled. The perceptual illusion that makes the operator experience the sensation of being there is called **telepresence.**

telephone gateway *noun*
    A telephone service that allows a subscriber using a regular telephone and a portable video terminal with a flip down keypad to tap into hundreds of online information and entertainment services, including games, news, stock market quotes, and shopping. Also called **gateway; information gateway.**

telepresence *noun*
    See TELEOPERATOR.

telepundit *noun*
    A television personality who makes comments or judgments in an authoritative manner. [Coined by William Safire of the *New York Times*]

temporarily able *adjective*
    Being neither disabled nor handicapped. A bias-free term. See TAB.

TENS *noun*
    A medical device that uses two or more electrical contacts to send an electrical current of 80 milliamps through the skin in order to interfere with the body's ability to perceive pain. [Acronym for **t**ranscutaneous **e**lectrical **n**erve **s**timulator]

teraflop *adjective*
    Of or relating to a computer's ability to calculate more than one trillion mathematical operations per second.

term limit law *noun*
A law that limits the number of terms elected representatives can serve. Some states, such as California, already have laws on how many years state legislators can serve, and the US Constitution has a term limit amendment allowing a president to serve no more than two terms.

terrorist art *noun*
An art genre characterized by violent imagery, abandonment of traditional forms, and mockery of traditional standards and practices of art. See OUTSIDER ART.

T4 cell *noun*
Any of a class of infection-fighting white blood cells, common to the skin and mucous membranes, that have become of interest in AIDS research. It is speculated that the AIDS virus attacks and infiltrates these cells, causing the virus to spread to other cells in the immune system.

THA *noun*
A pharmaceutical drug, tetrahydroaminoacridine, that is produced by Warner-Lambert and is being tested in the treatment of Alzheimer's disease. Also called **tacrine**.

thalassotherapy (thuh-LASS-oh-THER-uh-pee) *noun*
Holistic therapy using sea water showers, mud, seaweed, and algae baths, seaweed wraps, and other applications to the body that are reputed to be rich in vitamins and minerals and beneficial to skin and hair. [From Greek *thalassa* sea]

thalidomide (tha-LID-o-myde) *noun*
A drug that for years has been associated in the public mind with causing birth defects and has recently been put forward as being effective in the treatment of the potentially

fatal disease aplastic anemia and of some blood cancers and leprosy.

third market trading *noun*
The practice of trading, through off-exchange traders, stocks listed on an exchange.

thrash *noun*
The loudest, most raucous and dissonant form of heavy metal music. See GLAM; METAL FUNK; SPEED METAL.

throw shade *verb*
To shade.

thunderflash grenade *noun*
A grenade used in combating drug trafficking to create a diversion by producing a loud noise and brilliant light. Thunderflash grenades came to national attention when their use caused a fire in Minneapolis in which an innocent elderly couple were accidentally killed.

TICKS *noun*
Acronym for **T**wo-**I**ncome **C**ouple with **K**ids in **S**chool.

TIL cell *noun*
An extracted immune cell that shows promise as a cancer treatment. [From abbreviation of Tumor-Infiltrating Lymphocyte]

T.L.A.
Abbreviation of Three Letter Acronym.

TNF *noun*
A genetically engineered substance that has shown some promise in the treatment of certain types of cancer. [Abbre-

viation of tumor necrosis factor] Also called **tumor necrosis factor.**

tomahawk chop *noun*
A mock Indian war dance gesture performed at sports events and entertainments and regarded as offensive to Native Americans, who have protested its use as demeaning to their sacred rituals. Also called **chop.**

Tomorrow's Chair *noun*
A chair designed by Kristen Morrow that makes it easier for the disabled, arthritic, and elderly to rise from it to a standing position. When tipped slightly forward by the motion of its occupant, the chair reaches its unloading position entirely by nonmechanical means.

tonsil hockey *noun*
(*Slang*) Passionate kissing.

top-line growth *noun*
A new trend in picking growth stocks, emphasizing a company's top-line rather than bottom-line earnings growth. "A 'top-line' growth company has accelerating sales or revenue; revenue numbers are usually at the top of a company's income statement and list the amount of money received for goods or services sold. In the late 1980s, investors, fearing recession, over-indebtedness and other perils, were fixated on how fast a company's earnings — or 'bottom line' — grew." (Craig Torres, in the *Wall Street Journal*)

total quality *noun*
A plan in some corporate thinking for striving for near perfection at every level and in every endeavor. The total quality concept combines internal and external quality control and self-evaluation processes, in the form of new pro-

grams, development strategies, and managerial structures. Total quality has come under criticism as being hypothetically flawed and difficult if not impossible to achieve.

Touch Color code *noun*
A Braille-like system of raised symbols that allows the user to identify by touch specific signifiers for colors, shapes, and materials. The code is used to produce **Touch Books,** which are written in Braille and illustrated through Touch Color code symbols.

TQ2 *noun*
A beverage created by the inventor of Gatorade and containing a formulation that is alleged to improve exercise performance and extend workout time. [Abbreviation of thirst quencher two]

track ball *noun*
A device similar to the computer mouse in which the user rotates a small movable ball set in a stationary socket to cause the movement of the cursor on the screen. The track ball is said to be more efficient and accurate than the mouse.

trade dress *noun*
A characteristic combination of colors and patterns that become closely associated with a specific product or company, such as the red and white pattern of Marlboro cigarettes, the yellow and black design of Kodak products, or the sky blue logo of IBM.

transaction services *noun*
New telephone services that allow customers to manipulate information through use of the telephone or on a com-

puter screen. Shopping by computer, for example, is a transaction service.

trans fat *noun*
A fat contained in margarine that a recent study found can cause the blood levels of cholesterol to rise, although not as much as the saturated fats found in butter, according to the *Wellness Letter.*

transplant *noun*
A manufacturing facility that is set up in a foreign country where the products made are to be sold.

trash cash *noun*
Advertising leaflets that are designed to look like US currency, intentionally scattered on the well-traveled sidewalks of a city, and readily picked up by passersby, whose attention is caught by their resemblance to real money.

trash disco *noun*
A disco music featuring songs from the late 1970s performed either in their original versions or in newly recorded formats.

trash TV *noun*
See TABLOID TELEVISION.

trashvertising *noun*
Advertising through the use of trash cash and other materials that are aggressively handed out on busy streets and thrown away immediately by passers-by who pick them up. See TRASH CASH.

treadwall *noun*
See CLIMBING WALL.

trichosanthin *noun*
See COMPOUND Q.

Trinilite *noun*
An electronic television picture element made up of red, green, and blue cells and used as part of a larger screen. See JUMBOTRON.

trip *verb*
(*Slang*) To lie to, as in, "Are you tripping me about that?" An urban street term.

trom *noun*
(*Slang*) Marijuana. A urban street term.

true-blue green *noun*
A person who is fully committed to pro-environmental practices. [Derived from a study by the Roper Organization]

tubular *adjective*
(*Surfer Slang*) Really cool.

tumor necrosis factor *noun*
See TNF.

tuna laundering *noun*
The illegal practice of representing tuna as Dolphin Safe when it is not. See DOLPHIN SAFE.

turnaround *noun*
The status of a film or television project when its original sponsor passes on renewal and it becomes available to others for financing, syndication, or production.

turtle excluder device *noun*
See TED.

Tver (tuh-VEHR) *noun*
The Russian city formerly known as Kalinin.

tweet *noun*
(*Slang*) A teacher.

two-way television *noun*
An interactive television technology, recently approved by the Federal Communications Commission, that allows viewers' immediate response to and participation in TV viewing, as of game shows, and access to ordering food and paying bills. Also called **Interactive Video and Data Services; IVDS.**

tympanic thermometer *noun*
An infrared thermometer in which an accurate body temperature measurement is obtained in less than a minute through brief insertion into the patient's ear cavity.

Ubar *noun*
A recently discovered legendary lost city located at the base of the Qara mountains in the Arabian Peninsula and once renowned as an ancient trading metropolis.

Ukraine *noun*
A former constituent republic of the USSR that declared its independence after the dissolution of the Soviet Union. The capital city is Kiev.

ULDB *noun*

See MAXI-SLED. [Acronym for ultralight displacement boat]

unbundled stock unit *noun*

See USU.

unhappy camper *noun*

A discontented person, the opposite of a **happy camper**. Of unhappy camper, William Safire, in his "On Language" column, says, "the expression seems to have temporarily done away with the need for the modifiers *disgruntled, dissatisfied* and *discontented,* and substituted for the nouns *malcontent, grumbler, complainer, sorehead* and the more general *grouch.*"

universal mail box *noun*

A computer-controlled system consisting of paper mail and electronic mail messages processed and forwarded through voice-messaging technology and controlled by an automated attendant. See AUTOMATED ATTENDANT; VOICE MESSAGING.

unwelcome visit *noun*

(*British military*) A foray into enemy territory.

up-strength *adjective*

Of or relating to a new market segment of beer drinkers characterized by the brewing industry as having a propensity for higher strength brews: 4.5% alcohol beer as opposed to the traditional 3.5% brew.

UR *noun*

See UTILIZATION REVIEW.

USU *noun*

A new trading instrument that separates a share of stock into three components: one that turns a dividend into a bond, a second that turns capital appreciation into an option, and a third that gives investors the rights to any future dividend increases. [Abbreviation of unbundled stock units] Also called **unbundled stock unit.**

utilization review *noun*
A process of self-evaluation required by hospitals, HMOs, and health care facilities. Designed to assure the best patient care in the most cost-effective way, the utilization review is based on the premise that a team of multidisciplinary health care personnel, such as physicians, nurses, and administrators, can impartially assess service delivery and objectively measure its strengths and weaknesses. Also called **UR.**

UVA *noun*
A long wavelength constituent of sunlight that contributes to the aging of the skin. It penetrates deeply and may contribute to skin cancer. [Abbreviation of Ultraviolet A] See UVB.

UVB *noun*
A short wavelength constituent of sunlight that contributes to sunburn, premature aging, and wrinkling. It is largely responsible for basal cell and squamous cell carcinomas. [Abbreviation of Ultraviolet B] See UVA.

V

valspeak *noun*
A rather airy and bemused lingo associated with young people living in and around the southern California region generally known as "the valley."

value investing *noun*
The practice of making investment decisions by identifying stocks that sell for less than their perceived market valuation. The user of value investing tries to measure the true worth of the stock by using fundamental stock analysis.

veg out (vej) *verb*
To engage in passive activities; relax.

vidclip *noun*
A short film or section of tape in television for promotional purposes. [Short for *videoclip*]

videocart *noun*
A computerized shopping cart that displays advertisements. By means of an electronic liquid crystal display, the videocart can produce billboard-type advertising on a laptop size screen that is controlled through infrared and FM signals within the store.

video-dialtone *noun*
A new technology that allows subscribers to dial up video entertainment, as well as other information services, through fiber-optic wires that have been installed by the regional telephone company.

videographer *noun*
The equivalent, in a video production, of a film's cinematographer.

video jukebox *noun*
A cable channel that airs rock videos by request. Viewers call a 900 number, for which they are charged, and punch

in a request code using the touch tone keys on their phone pads.

videolaseroscopy (vɪd-ee-oh-lay-zer-os-kuh-pee) *noun*
Videoscope surgery within the abdomen. "Dr. Camran Nezhat described his experience with videolaseroscopy for the treatment of endometriosis and . . . periovarian adhesions." (*Ob.Gyn.News*)

video on demand *noun*
A planned new service that would allow subscribers to choose from a large range of viewing products at any given time; an extension of the pay-per-view service, but with far greater flexibility.

videophile *noun*
An expert on or collector of videotapes.

videophone *noun*
A proposed new phone system that will allow subscribers to see as well as hear each other over phone lines.

videoscope surgery *noun*
Any of various new surgical techniques that employ a slender fiber-optic tube containing a light source, miniature video camera, telescopic lens, and VCR, as well as surgical cutters, graspers, and staplers. The tube is inserted into the patient through a tiny incision, enabling the surgeon to reach and operate on areas deep inside the body while watching what he or she is doing on a high-resolution video monitor. Also called **videosurgery.**

videowindow *noun*
A new telecommunications technology that makes it possible during teleconferencing to see people in a remote loca-

tion as clearly as if they were in the same room. "To make the videowindow picture appear real, the system uses mirrors to merge images from two cameras into one panoramic view that has twice the density of ordinary video." (*New York Times*)

videozine *noun*
A new publishing medium in which a magazine is recorded and circulated on video cassette. For example, *Travelquest* is a videozine for travel agents that consists of soft-sell commercials, brief travelogues, and useful information for both the agent and the client.

vidisk *noun*
A videodisk.

virtual classroom *noun*
See DISTANCE EDUCATION.

virtual-86 mode *noun*
A method for running the Intel-based computer chips that allows programs to perform multiple tasks at the same time. See DOS EXTENDER; PROTECTED MODE.

virtual reality *noun*
See ARTIFICIAL REALITY.

visionary art *noun*
See OUTSIDER ART.

vision quest *noun*
A practice advocated in some religious circles that requires practitioners to undergo intense solitude, fasting, and introspection as ways of coming into contact with deep,

spiritual parts of themselves that can serve to direct their
religious and spiritual growth.

Vladikavkaz (vla-duh-kaf-KAZ) *noun*
The Russian city formerly known as Ordzhonikidze.

voice annotation *noun*
A new computer technology that allows a person to put
spoken comments at appropriate places in a report, letter,
memo, or any other written document that appears on the
computer screen. The voice annotation allows a user to
make comments while reading the text on screen and
allows the comments to be carried along with the document
for its subsequent revisions.

voice messaging *noun*
A form of voice mail in which messages and their responses can be forwarded, recorded, and responded to elec-
tronically through the use of voice-recognition computer
technology. See AUTOMATED ATTENDANT.

voice-stress analysis *noun*
A relatively new type of lie detector test that is based on
an electronic analysis of the person's voice while answering
questions or describing a situation. The results are not ad-
missible in court.

voluntary enhanced exit program *noun*
A program for eliminating people from jobs in a company
by giving them attractive incentives to leave.

VSP *noun*
See MICROCAR. [From *voiture sans permis*, car without
license]

vulture fund *noun*
An investment vehicle that buys shares, equity, or bonds in debt-burdened companies or busted properties. The investments are undertaken with the intention of later reselling them for significant profit during a market turnaround.

Vyatka (vee-AHT-kuh) *noun*
The Russian city formerly known as Kirov.

W

··········

wa (wah) *noun*
A Japanese term for a sense of team spirit that requires all individual goals to be subordinated to the ultimate interest of the team.

Wagyu bull (WAG-yoo) *noun*
Any of a breed of black cattle originally from Japan but now also raised in the United States. Fed a special diet and given regular massages, they produce an exceptionally tender and flavorful beef known in Japan as **Wagyu meat** and in the United States as **Kobe beef.**

wake-up call *noun*
A portentous event, report, or situation that brings an issue to immediate attention. "To the treasurer of Massachusetts, it's the recession that sends a wake-up call to state governments." (*New York Times*) "It's time to send a wake-up call to advertisers that not all trade promotion spending is going to line the pockets of retailers." (*Advertising Age*)

wakilana *adjective*
(*Slang*) Crazy; wacky.

walking pump *noun*
A woman's dress shoe that combines features of a sneaker and a high heel.

warehouse club *noun*
A retail store that has features of a discount store, a buying club, and a wholesaler. Members pay an annual fee to shop and are allowed to purchase bulk merchandise at almost wholesale prices.

waterwalking *noun*
An aerobic and toning exercise consisting of a brisk stroll through the shallow part of a body of water, such as a pool, lake, pond, bay, or even an ocean. When waterwalking, a person burns between 300 and 500 calories per hour, considerably more calories than by land walking, and at the same time places less stress on the supportive muscles.

waterworld *noun*
An amusement complex emphasizing water-based rides and activities.

wearable computer *noun*
Any of various small computers that can be easily carried around or even slipped in a pocket, as for use on train and plane trips. See PALMTOP COMPUTER; POWERBOOK.

web issue *noun*
A social or economic issue in a political campaign that brings together different interest groups within the party and musters support for the party's candidate. See WEDGE ISSUE.

wedge issue *noun*
A political campaign issue, such as reducing or increasing social security benefits, that can figuratively drive a wedge between different voting segments of the opposing party, allowing one's own candidate to capitalize on the resulting dissension and gain otherwise unobtainable votes. [Term originated by the late political strategist Lee Atwater] See WEB ISSUE.

Weed and Seed *noun*
A two-stage model for federal spending in urban areas, part of the Bush administration's 1993 budget proposal, in which money would first be allocated to weed out drug dealers and organized crime in a defined area, and then seed money would be provided for community agencies to underwrite education, health care, housing, and job training.

weightism *noun*
Discrimination and oppression of the obese by the trim. A bias-free term. See NONSIZIST.

wellness program *noun*
A corporate- or government-sponsored program promoting a wide variety of preventive physical and mental health measures, including stress reduction, smoking cessation, physical fitness and exercise, and blood pressure monitoring and control.

wetwork *noun*
An espionage assignment that calls for murder. [From *Wetwork*, a novel by Christopher Buckley]

whack *verb*
(*Slang*) To kill (someone); knock off. An underworld term that came to public prominence during the 1992 trial of mobster John Gotti.

whistle-blower law *noun*

A law that protects an employee who reports corporate, governmental, or organizational wrongdoing to appropriate authorities and that allows the whistle blower to share in any recovery or savings that results from the report.

white hat *noun*

A person seen as playing a virtuous role in a political scandal. See BLACK HAT.

whitemail *noun*

An investment strategy whereby a major investor develops a close relationship with an underperforming company whose managers fear takeover or ouster, the investor defending the management from raiders by buying a significant block of the company's voting stock, usually at an advantageous price. This strategy is the opposite of **greenmail,** whereby the company would pay corporate raiders large sums to leave them alone.

white-right movement *noun*

The white supremacist groups in the nation regarded collectively.

wifeable *adjective*

(Of audio equipment) Designed and styled with a minimum of technological gadgetry, so as to please women. The retrograde and presumably male assumption is that women will be guided by aesthetics rather than an interest in technology in making a choice.

Willie Horton *verb*

To attack (a political candidate) with advertising that plays on racial fears. [From the television commercials run by the Republicans in the 1988 presidential campaign against Democratic candidate Michael Dukakis of Massachusetts, in which Willie Horton, a Black Massachusetts convict who raped a woman while out of prison on the state's furlough program, was depicted as an example of Dukakis's indifference to the public welfare]

Wilma *noun*
(*Surfer Slang*) A scatterbrained woman. [From the 1960s television cartoon show *The Flintstones*] See BARNEY.

Windows *noun*
An advanced graphics-based proprietary operating system for IBM-compatible computers developed and marketed by Microsoft Corporation as a replacement for the older DOS system. See OS/2.

windshield tourist *noun*
A touring motorist who rarely leaves the car to enjoy the sights.

wine dinner *noun*
A restaurant promotional scheme, often organized and promoted in conjunction with a wine importer or producer, in which a variety of preselected wines are served with the courses of a dinner and included in the dinner's price. "Wine dinners like those at the Four Seasons attract people who know their vintages. But wine dinners are particularly appealing to people who like wine but don't know one label from another." (*New York Times*)

winter blues *noun*
A medically recognized form of depression associated with the shorter days of winter and recently treated by using special lights mimicking sunlight to fool the victim's body

into believing it is summer rather than winter. Also called **SAD; seasonal affective disorder; seasonal depression.**

wireless cable *noun*
A form of broadcasting through microwave frequencies. Intended as a competitor for cable television systems, wireless cable shares the frequencies used by educational services and university-based television stations.

wiseguy *noun*
See GOODFELLA.

wise-use movement *noun*
A movement founded in reaction to the political strength of the environmental lobby and led by business groups, industrial lobbyists, and investors who caution voters in upcoming elections to consider the long-range impact of environmental measures on jobs, on the economy, and on personal property rights.

wobble motor *noun*
A newly developed aluminum and stainless steel micromotor that consists of a tiny rod that rotates inside the shaft with a slight wobbling movement. "Its developers at the university [of Utah]'s Center for Engineering Design say that because the motor wobbles rather than rotating smoothly, there is less friction." (*New York Times*) See MICROMACHINE; MICROMOTOR.

wolf-pack robbery *noun*
A robbery committed by a roving gang of marauders who seem randomly to pick one victim and then rapidly move on to another.

woman of size *noun*
A heavy woman. A bias-free term.

womanspirit *noun*
A feminist doctrine that rejects the traditional male-centered authority and imagery that is characteristic of most religions and emphasizes a feminist spirituality in all aspects of religious belief and practice, from the conceptualization of the deity to the role and staffing of clergy.

woolly adelgid *noun*
A brownish-red oval insect, about 1/32nd of an inch in length, that feeds on hemlock trees and has been found increasingly in the northeast US.

woopie *noun*
A person of comfortable means who is over 65. [Acronym for **w**ell-**o**ff **o**lder **p**erson + ie (as in yuppie)]

world band *adjective*
The international shortwave radio frequencies that, because of digital tuning, are being monitored increasingly around the world.

world-beat music *noun*
A popular music with roots in African music that usually has non-English lyrics addressing both local problems and universal concerns and is marked by lively rhythm and instrumentation.

world music *noun*
Indigenous Third World music that over the past five years has experienced increasing commercial viability in the US and Europe.

wrap account *noun*
An investment service in which a money manager, for a percentage fee, makes all the investment decisions for an individual investor.

Y

YABA *noun*
Acronym for **Y**et **A**nother **B**loody **A**cronym. Used especially by computer hackers and those in the marketing and advertising ends of the computer industry.

yabba-dabba-doo *interjection*
(*Surfer Slang*) Used as a greeting. [From the cartoon show *The Flintstones*]

Yekaterinburg (yi-KAT-uh-ruhn-berg) *noun*
The Russian city formerly known as Sverdlovsk.

yield management *noun*
A technologically advanced management technique based on sophisticated computer software by which a manufacturing company can implement its pricing policy, rebates, and discounting according to a variety of subtle and rapidly changing variables. The yield management calculations take into account such factors as market conditions, regional costs, promotional expenses, employee salaries, competition, and other factors that figure in the equation.

yokozuna (yoh-koh-zoo-nah) *noun*
The grand champion status in Japan in Sumo wrestling, which has been awarded only to about 60 wrestlers in the

sport's 300-year history. Yokozuna became an international subject of controversy in 1992 when Konishiki, an American citizen, was denied yokozuna in Japan, despite his unsurpassed success in the sport.

yuppie flu *noun*
(*Informal*) A medical condition generalized to include chronic fatigue syndrome, chronic fatigue and immune dysfunction syndrome, mononucleosis, and the Epstein–Barr virus syndrome.

Z

zap art *noun*
Art in the form of circulars and other leaflets created to raise awareness about and stir interest in pressing social issues, such as animal rights and global warming.

zein (ZEEN) *noun*
A protein derived from corn kernels that, because it has many characteristics of a fat, can be used in foods and in cooking as a low-calorie fat substitute. One advantage of zein over synthetic fat substitutes, according to Dr. Arun Kilara, a professor of food science at Pennsylvania State University, is that it has better "mouth feel" than the synthetics.

zero-cost collars *noun*
A failed Wall Street hedging strategy of late 1991. In the zero-cost collars strategy, to lock into heavy stock gains, brokers recommended a futures and options strategy that

would put a "collar" of 20% gains on a portfolio. When the market turned up suddenly in December, investors missed out on greater gains, to their chagrin.

zip city *noun*

(*Slang*) Nothing; zero: "Bush–Quayle campaign spokeswoman Torie Clarke dismissed Perot's remarks as 'baloney' and conspiracy fantasies. Asked if the Bush campaign has leaked any negative stuff on Perot, she replied: 'Zip city.' " (Deborah Orin, *New York Post*)

z-lot *noun*

A house-siting design, first used in Europe but now popular in the US, in which detached homes with garages are built on staggered narrow lots, allowing greater building density. A Baltimore developer was able to build 118 homes on 37 acres, compared with 80 with conventional siting, according to Larry Carson of the *New York Times*.

zup *interjection*

(*Surfer Slang*) Used interrogatively as a contraction of "What's up?"

Index

**Arts and
Entertainment**

stock basket
stockout cost
stock parking
stub stock
stuff
sunk cost
synthetic floater
telemedia
third market trad-
 ing
top-line growth
transplant
unbundled stock
 unit
USU
value investing
videocart
voluntary enhanced
 exit program
vulture fund
wa
wellness program
whistle-blower law
whitemail
wrap account
yield management
zero-cost collars

**Causes and
Movements**

ableist language
abortuary
acceptional child
Agenda 21
animal companion
animalist
animal lookism

bad hejab
biocentrism
bioreserve
brain birth
Chabad
chop
communitarianism
companion animal
conscious con-
 nected breathing
cruelty-free
cultural genocide
cultural jammer
deathbelt
demarketing
differently abled
Dolphin Safe
dowry death
DWEM
eco-babble
eco-justice
eco-ranching
equity gap
Flashmora
flesh
fundies
generously cut
good hejab
greenback green
green lobby
green product
greenway move-
 ment
grouser
helium heels
ice people
jammer
lookism
LULUs

maintenance hatch
Manglish
megachurch
motivationally de-
 ficient
Noah Principle
nonsizist
out
phallocentrism
Pink Angel
PLAN
pre-woman
privileging
rebirthing
rescue
sex worker
Sheilaism
shepherding
social marketing
sun people
temporarily able
tomahawk chop
vision quest
wise-use move-
 ment
womanspirit
zap art

Computers

animatronic toy
Anonymous Call
 Rejection
architectural crisis
artificial reality
artware
Bernoulli box
blocking